cook & enjoy

Baking

cook & enjoy

Baking

Delicious recipes for the everyday cook

This edition published by Parragon Books Ltd in 2016

LOVE FOOD is an imprint of Parragon Books Ltd

Parragon Books Ltd
Chartist House
15–17 Trim Street
Bath BA1 1HA, UK
www.parragon.com/lovefood

ISBN 978-1-4748-4397-3

Printed in China

Cover photography by Charlie Richards
Cover home economy by Mima Sinclair
Introduction by Linda Doeser

Notes for the Reader
This book uses both metric and imperial measurements. Follow the same units of measurement throughout; do not mix metric and imperial. All spoon measurements are level: teaspoons are assumed to be 5 ml, and tablespoons are assumed to be 15 ml. Unless otherwise stated, milk is assumed to be full fat, eggs and individual vegetables are medium, pepper is freshly ground black pepper and salt is table salt. Unless otherwise stated, all root vegetables should be peeled prior to using.

The times given are an approximate guide only. Preparation times differ according to the techniques used by different people and the cooking times may also vary from those given.

Cover image shows the Clementine Cake on page 50.

contents

Introduction

The aroma of warm bread straight from the oven or a freshly baked cake must be one of the most appetizing and evocative smells in the world. Home-made muffins, cupcakes and biscuits make the perfect any-time snack, while a luxurious layered gateau is the crowning glory of any celebration meal. Whether it's a batch of scones that can be whipped up in moments by even an inexperienced cook, or a melt-in-the-mouth pastry that needs a light touch and rather more time, there is something very special about home-baked treats.

Baking is one of the most satisfying kinds of cooking, but for some reason it has a reputation for being time-consuming and complicated. This couldn't be further from the truth – muffins, cupcakes, brownies, bars and biscuits take very little time and, providing you follow a few basic rules, the results will always be far more appealing and much tastier than anything you can buy. New twists on family favourites combine innovation and tradition, while anyone with a creative urge can really push the boat out with fabulous iced, layered and chocolate-topped confections that look almost too lovely to eat. Baking can be wonderfully therapeutic, too – if you're feeling a little fed up, why not work off your frustrations by kneading some bread dough and then bask in the warm glow of self-satisfaction as you cut the first delicious slice of the loaf? Of course, not everyone has a sweet tooth and, in any event, there are many occasions when savouries are the order of the day. There's something so much more rewarding about serving home-made tartlets, crackers and mini quiches instead of the more usual peanuts and crisps. However, be warned that your home-baked delicacies, sweet or savoury, are not likely to hang around for very long and you will soon become the most popular host in the neighbourhood.

Top tips for success

Keep an eye on 'use-by' dates. If kept too long, flour and nuts will go rancid, dried fruit will become mouldy, spices will lose their aroma and flavour, and yeast will die.

Precise measurement of ingredients is more important with baking than with any other kind of cooking and makes the difference between success and failure. If the proportions of fat, flour and egg, for example, are incorrect, a cake will be heavy and doughy.

Don't substitute ingredients. Different flours vary in their characteristics, particularly in the quantity of liquid they will absorb. As a general rule, plain flour is used for pastry doughs; self-raising flour, which includes added baking powder, for cakes and scones; and strong flour, with its high gluten content, for bread. The most commonly used fat is butter, not least because it has the richest flavour. Firm margarine, sold in blocks, lacks the flavour of butter but may be used in the same way. Soft margarine, sold in tubs, is specified in some recipes. However, do not use low-fat spreads as these simply do not work with most cakes and pastries.

With the exception of pastry doughs, which should be kept as cool as possible, all forms of baking work better if all the ingredients have been brought to room temperature before you start. Remove eggs and fat from the refrigerator about 30 minutes in advance.

Pastry doughs should be handled as little as possible and kept cool. Put the mixing bowl and a jug of water into the refrigerator to chill 30 minutes beforehand. Rinse your hands in cold water (and dry them thoroughly) before rubbing fat into flour, or use a pastry blender. Grating the fat into the flour reduces the amount of time required for rubbing in and is a good trick on a hot day. A marble slab and rolling pin are ideal for rolling out the dough as they help keep it cool.

Pastry doughs should always be rested in the refrigerator before rolling out. This enables the gluten, a protein in the flour that starts to react when the liquid is added, to become firm and elastic. This makes the dough easy to roll out and helps to prevent it shrinking during cooking.

Many people are hesitant about using yeast and so don't make bread, but these days you can't go wrong with easy-blend dried yeast. This concentrated dried yeast is added with the dry ingredients – flour and salt, for example – and there is no need to mix it with water first. Fresh and ordinary dried yeast must be activated before they are used.

Always use the size and shape of tin specified in the recipe, especially when making cakes. If the tin is too large, the cake will be flat; if it is too small, the centre will bulge or the mixture will run over the sides. Some recipes give the tin's capacity – to find this simply use a measuring jug to pour water into the tin and note how much water it takes to fill it.

Preheat the oven to the required temperature and avoid opening the oven door during baking, especially with cakes, as the sudden draught of colder air will make them collapse. Use a timer to estimate when the cake is likely to be cooked and test by inserting a fine skewer into the centre. If it comes out clean,

the cake is ready. Test sponge cakes by pressing the top lightly with your finger; it should spring back immediately and the cake should have shrunk slightly from the sides of the tin. Bread can be tested by tapping it on the base – it will sound hollow when it is cooked.

Follow the recipe instructions for cooling. Light cakes are turned out onto a wire rack 3–5 minutes after they come out of the oven and while they are still warm, but heavy cakes are best left to cool in the tin. Some delicate biscuits should be left on the baking trays to firm up before being transferred to a wire rack. Always use a wire rack to allow air to circulate to prevent cakes, biscuits and loaves becoming soggy.

shortcrust pastry

makes 225 g/8 oz

225 g/8 oz plain flour, plus extra for dusting
115 g/4 oz butter, chilled
2–3 tbsp cold water

STEP 1. Sift the flour into a bowl. Cut the butter into small cubes and add to the flour. Rub in using your fingertips, lifting your hands high above the bowl to incorporate more air. The mixture will resemble fine breadcrumbs when the butter has been fully rubbed in. Gradually add the water and use your fingers to bring the dough together.

STEP 2. Alternatively, use a food processor to make the pastry. Put the flour and butter in the bowl of the processor and process until the mixture resembles fine breadcrumbs. At this stage, you can either add the water to the processor and process until the pastry comes together, or tip the flour and butter mixture into a bowl and mix in the water by hand.

STEP 3. Turn out the dough onto a lightly floured work surface and knead very lightly. The pastry should be wrapped in clingfilm and chilled in the refrigerator for 30 minutes before rolling.

puff pastry

makes 350 g/12 oz

350 g/12 oz plain flour
175 g/6 oz butter
8 tbsp cold water

STEP 1. Sift the flour into a bowl and rub in 40 g/1½ oz of the butter. Add the water and use your fingers to bring the mixture together. Knead briefly to form a smooth dough. Put in a polythene bag and chill for 30 minutes.

STEP 2. Roll out the remaining butter between two sheets of clingfilm to form a block about 1 cm/½ inch thick. Roll out the dough to a square about four times the size of the block of butter. Put the block of butter in the centre of the dough and fold over the corners of the dough to completely enclose the butter. Roll out the dough into a rectangle three times as long as it is wide. Fold over a third of the dough to cover the middle third, then fold the remainder over the top. Give the dough a half turn, roll out to form another rectangle and fold again as before. Repeat the initial rolling and folding six times in total, chilling the dough between each rolling.

STEP 3. Chill the dough for a final 30 minutes, then use as required.

cakes

chocolate slab cake

Serves 9

Difficulty: Medium

Prep: 20 mins, plus cooling and setting

Cook: 55 mins–1 hour

INGREDIENTS

200 g/7 oz unsalted butter, plus extra for greasing

100 g/3½ oz plain chocolate, broken into pieces

5 tbsp water

350 g/12 oz plain flour

2 tsp baking powder

250 g/9 oz soft light brown sugar

5 tbsp soured cream

2 eggs, beaten

ICING

200 g/7 oz plain chocolate, broken into pieces

6 tbsp water

3 tbsp single cream

15 g/½ oz unsalted butter, chilled

STEP 1. Preheat the oven to 190°C/375°F/Gas Mark 5. Grease a 23-cm/9-inch square cake tin and line the base with baking paper.

STEP 2. Melt the butter and chocolate with the water in a saucepan over a low heat, stirring frequently. Sift the flour and baking powder into a mixing bowl and stir in the sugar. Pour in the chocolate mixture and beat well until all of the ingredients are evenly mixed. Stir in the soured cream, followed by the eggs.

STEP 3. Pour the mixture into the prepared tin. Bake in the preheated oven for 40–45 minutes until springy to the touch.

STEP 4. Leave the cake to cool slightly in the tin, then turn out onto a wire rack and leave to cool completely.

STEP 5. To make the icing, melt the chocolate with the water in a saucepan over a very low heat, stir in the cream and remove from the heat. Stir in the butter, then pour the icing over the cooled cake, using a palette knife to spread it evenly over the top. Leave to set before slicing.

chocolate & orange semolina cake

Serves 8

Difficulty: Medium

Prep: 30 mins, plus cooling
Cook: 35–40 mins

INGREDIENTS

1 large orange

100 g/3½ oz caster sugar

2 eggs

85 g/3 oz unsalted butter, melted, plus extra for greasing

175 g/6 oz semolina

55 g/2 oz cocoa powder

1½ tsp baking powder

icing sugar, for dusting

STEP 1. Preheat the oven to 180°C/350°F/Gas Mark 4. Grease a 20-cm/8-inch round cake tin and line the base with baking paper.

STEP 2. Coarsely grate the rind from the orange and reserve. With a sharp knife, cut away all the remaining peel and white pith, then cut the flesh into small pieces, reserving the juices.

STEP 3. Put the sugar and eggs into a mixing bowl and whisk vigorously with a hand-held electric mixer until pale and foamy. Gradually whisk in the melted butter, pouring in a thin steady stream as you whisk. Sift in the semolina, cocoa powder and baking powder and fold in lightly and evenly. Stir in the orange pieces with their juices and mix to a soft batter.

STEP 4. Spoon the batter into the prepared tin and smooth the surface with a palette knife. Bake in the preheated oven for 35–40 minutes until just firm to the touch. Leave to cool in the tin for 5 minutes, then turn out onto a wire rack to cool completely.

STEP 5. Scatter the cooled cake with the reserved grated orange rind and dust with icing sugar.

marbled chocolate & vanilla ring

Serves 12

Difficulty: Medium

Prep: 20 mins, plus cooling

Cook: 45–50 mins

INGREDIENTS

oil or melted butter,
  for greasing

175 g/6 oz plain flour

1 tbsp baking powder

175 g/6 oz unsalted butter,
  softened

175 g/6 oz caster sugar

3 eggs, beaten

2 tbsp cocoa powder

2 tbsp milk

1 tsp vanilla extract

icing sugar, for dusting

STEP 1. Preheat the oven to 160°C/325°F/Gas Mark 3. Grease a 1.5-litre/2½-pint ring cake tin, preferably non-stick.

STEP 2. Sift the flour and baking powder into a mixing bowl and add the butter, caster sugar and eggs. Beat well until smooth. Transfer half the mixture to a separate bowl.

STEP 3. Mix the cocoa powder with the milk and stir into one bowl of mixture. Add the vanilla extract to the other bowl and mix evenly. Spoon alternate tablespoons of the two mixtures into the prepared tin and lightly swirl with a palette knife for a marbled effect.

STEP 4. Bake in the preheated oven for 40–50 minutes, or until risen, firm and golden brown. Leave to cool in the tin for 10 minutes, then turn out onto a wire rack to cool completely. Dust with icing sugar just before serving.

*Note: Marbling produces maximum impact for minimum effort. For best results, don't be too heavy-handed when swirling the mixtures together – you want to keep a nice contrast.

victoria sponge cake

Serves 8–10

Difficulty: Medium

Prep: 25 mins, plus cooling
Cook: 25–30 mins

INGREDIENTS

175 g/6 oz unsalted butter, softened, plus extra for greasing

175 g/6 oz caster sugar

3 eggs, beaten

175 g/6 oz self-raising flour

pinch of salt

3 tbsp raspberry jam

1 tbsp icing sugar

STEP 1. Preheat the oven to 180°C/350°F/Gas Mark 4. Grease two 20-cm/8-inch sandwich tins and line the bases with baking paper.

STEP 2. Put the butter and caster sugar into a mixing bowl and cream together until light and fluffy. Add the eggs a little at a time, beating well after each addition. Sift the flour and salt into a separate bowl and carefully add to the mixture, folding in with a metal spoon or a spatula.

STEP 3. Divide the mixture between the prepared tins and smooth the surface with the spatula. Place the tins on the same shelf in the centre of the preheated oven and bake for 25–30 minutes until well risen, golden brown and beginning to shrink from the sides of the tins.

STEP 4. Leave to cool in the tins for 1 minute, then turn out onto a wire rack to cool completely. Sandwich together the cooled cakes with the jam and dust with the icing sugar.

jewel-topped madeira cake

Serves 8–10

Difficulty: Medium

Prep: 20 mins, plus cooling
Cook: 1½–1¾ hours

INGREDIENTS

225 g/8 oz unsalted butter, softened, plus extra for greasing

225 g/8 oz golden caster sugar

finely grated rind of 1 lemon

4 eggs, beaten

350 g/12 oz self-raising flour, sifted

2–3 tbsp milk

FRUIT TOPPING

2½ tbsp clear honey

300 g/10½ oz glacé fruit, sliced

STEP 1. Preheat the oven to 160°C/325°F/Gas Mark 3. Grease a 20-cm/8-inch round cake tin and line with baking paper.

STEP 2. Put the butter, sugar and lemon rind into a mixing bowl and cream together until light and fluffy. Gradually beat in the eggs. Gently fold in the flour, adding enough of the milk to give a soft dropping consistency.

STEP 3. Spoon the mixture into the prepared tin. Bake in the preheated oven for 1½–1¾ hours until risen and golden and a skewer inserted into the centre comes out clean. Leave to cool in the tin for 10 minutes, then turn out onto a wire rack and leave to cool completely.

STEP 4. To make the topping, brush the honey over the top of the cake and arrange the glacé fruit on top.

honey & almond cake

Serves 8

Difficulty: Medium

Prep: 20 mins, plus 2 hours cooling
Cook: 1 hour

INGREDIENTS

75 g/2¾ oz soft margarine,
  plus extra for greasing

75 g/2¾ oz soft light brown
  sugar

2 eggs

175 g/6 oz self-raising flour

1 tsp baking powder

4 tbsp milk

2 tbsp clear honey

50 g/1¾ oz flaked almonds

SYRUP

225 g/8 oz clear honey

2 tbsp lemon juice

STEP 1. Preheat the oven to 180°C/350°F/Gas Mark 4. Grease an 18-cm/7-inch round cake tin and line with baking paper.

STEP 2. Put the margarine, sugar, eggs, flour, baking powder, milk and honey into a large mixing bowl and beat well with a wooden spoon for about 1 minute, or until all the ingredients are thoroughly mixed together.

STEP 3. Spoon into the prepared tin, smooth the surface with the back of a spoon or a knife and sprinkle with the flaked almonds.

STEP 4. Bake in the preheated oven for about 50 minutes, or until well risen and a skewer inserted into the centre comes out clean.

STEP 5. Meanwhile, make the syrup. Combine the honey and lemon juice in a small saucepan and simmer over a low heat for about 5 minutes, or until the syrup coats the back of a spoon.

STEP 6. Remove the cake from the oven and pour the syrup over it, allowing it to soak into the cake. Leave the cake to cool in the tin for at least 2 hours before slicing.

coconut & lime cake

Serves 8

Difficulty: Medium

Prep: 30 mins, plus cooling and setting
Cook: 1–1¼ hours

INGREDIENTS

175 g/6 oz unsalted butter, softened, plus extra for greasing

175 g/6 oz caster sugar

3 eggs, beaten

150 g/5½ oz self-raising flour

85 g/3 oz desiccated coconut

grated rind and juice of 1 lime

25 g/1 oz shredded coconut, lightly toasted

ICING

175 g/6 oz icing sugar

grated rind and juice of 1 lime

STEP 1. Preheat the oven to 160°C/325°F/Gas Mark 3. Grease a 20-cm/8-inch round cake tin and line with baking paper.

STEP 2. Put the butter and sugar into a mixing bowl and cream together until light and fluffy. Gradually beat in the eggs. Sift in the flour and gently fold in using a metal spoon. Fold in the desiccated coconut, lime rind and juice.

STEP 3. Spoon the mixture into the prepared tin and level the surface. Bake in the preheated oven for 1–1¼ hours until risen, golden and firm to the touch. Leave to cool in the tin for 5 minutes, then turn out onto a wire rack to cool completely.

STEP 4. To make the icing, sift the icing sugar into a bowl. Stir in the lime rind and juice to make a thick, smooth icing, adding a few drops of water, if necessary. Spoon the icing over the top of the cake, allowing it to drizzle down the sides of the cake. Scatter the shredded coconut over the icing and leave to set.

coffee streusel cake

Serves 8–10

Difficulty: Medium

Prep: 30 mins, plus cooling

Cook: 50 mins–1 hour

INGREDIENTS

225 g/8 oz plain flour

1 tbsp baking powder

70 g/2½ oz caster sugar

150 ml/5 fl oz milk

2 eggs

115 g/4 oz unsalted butter, melted and cooled, plus extra for greasing

2 tbsp instant coffee granules, dissolved in 1 tbsp boiling water

50 g/1¾ oz chopped almonds

icing sugar, for dusting

TOPPING

70 g/2½ oz self-raising flour

70 g/2½ oz demerara sugar

25 g/1 oz unsalted butter, cut into small pieces

1 tsp mixed spice

1 tbsp water

STEP 1. Preheat the oven to 190°C/375°F/Gas Mark 5. Grease a 23-cm/9-inch round loose-based cake tin and line with baking paper.

STEP 2. Sift the plain flour and baking powder into a mixing bowl, then stir in the caster sugar.

STEP 3. Whisk together the milk, eggs, melted butter and coffee mixture and pour onto the dry ingredients. Add the almonds and lightly mix together. Spoon the mixture into the prepared tin.

STEP 4. To make the topping, mix the self-raising flour and demerara sugar together in a bowl. Rub in the butter with your fingertips until the mixture resembles breadcrumbs. Sprinkle in the mixed spice and water and bring the mixture together in loose crumbs.

STEP 5. Sprinkle the topping evenly over the cake and bake in the preheated oven for 50 minutes–1 hour. Cover loosely with foil if the topping is browning too quickly.

STEP 6. Leave to cool in the tin. Remove the cake from the tin and dust with icing sugar just before serving.

glazed fruit & nut cake

Serves 16–18

Difficulty: Medium

Prep: 25 mins, plus cooling and setting
Cook: 1 hour

INGREDIENTS

oil or melted butter,
  for greasing

250 g/9 oz plain flour, plus
  extra for dusting

1 tbsp baking powder

1 tsp mixed spice

175 g/6 oz unsalted butter,
  softened

175 g/6 oz dark muscovado
  sugar

3 eggs, beaten

1 tsp vanilla extract

2 tbsp milk

300 g/10½ oz mixed
  dried fruit

85 g/3 oz chopped
  mixed nuts

TO DECORATE

3 tbsp clear honey, warmed

350 g/12 oz mixed glacé
  fruits, such as pineapple,
  cherries and orange

55 g/2 oz whole shelled nuts,
  such as Brazil nuts, almonds
  and walnuts

STEP 1. Preheat the oven to 160°C/325°F/Gas Mark 3. Grease a 23-cm/9-inch round springform cake tin and dust with a little flour, shaking out the excess.

STEP 2. Sift the flour, baking powder and mixed spice into a mixing bowl and add the butter, sugar, eggs and vanilla extract. Beat well until smooth, then stir in the milk, dried fruit and chopped nuts.

STEP 3. Spoon the mixture into the prepared tin and smooth the surface with a palette knife. Bake in the preheated oven for about 1 hour, or until risen, firm and golden brown.

STEP 4. Leave to cool in the tin for 30 minutes, then unclip and remove the springform and transfer the cake to a wire rack to cool completely.

STEP 5. To decorate, brush the top of the cake with a little of the warmed honey, then arrange the glacé fruits and whole shelled nuts on top. Brush with the remaining honey and leave to set.

date & spice loaf

Serves 8–10

Difficulty: Easy

Prep: 20 mins, plus cooling
Cook: 40–50 mins

INGREDIENTS

oil or melted butter,
 for greasing

85 g/3 oz plain white flour

100 g/3½ oz plain wholemeal
 flour

1 tbsp baking powder

1 tsp mixed spice

175 g/6 oz unsalted butter,
 softened

175 g/6 oz golden caster
 sugar

3 eggs, beaten

1 tsp vanilla extract

175 g/6 oz stoned dates,
 roughly chopped

STEP 1. Preheat the oven to 160°C/325°F/Gas Mark 3. Grease and line a 1.3-litre/2¼-pint loaf tin.

STEP 2. Sift the white flour, wholemeal flour, baking powder and mixed spice into a mixing bowl, adding any bran left in the sieve. Add the butter, sugar, eggs and vanilla extract and beat well until smooth, then stir in half the dates.

STEP 3. Spoon the mixture into the prepared tin and scatter over the remaining dates. Bake in the preheated oven for 40–50 minutes, or until the cake is risen, firm and golden brown.

STEP 4. Leave to cool in the tin for 10 minutes, then turn out onto a wire rack and leave to cool completely.

*Note: This delicious spiced fruit loaf is one of the original 'cut-and-come-again' cakes. It can also be served at teatime as a bread, with plenty of butter for spreading. If it's more than a couple of days old, toast it first — simply delicious!

gingerbread with lemon drizzle

Serves 9

Difficulty: Medium

Prep: 25 mins, plus cooling and setting
Cook: 25–30 mins

INGREDIENTS

butter, for greasing

175 g/6 oz self-raising flour

1 tbsp ground ginger

2 eggs

100 g/3½ oz light muscovado
sugar

4 tbsp black treacle

4 tbsp milk

4 tbsp sunflower oil

TO DECORATE

100 g/3½ oz icing sugar

½ tsp lemon extract

1 tbsp silver dragées

STEP 1. Preheat the oven to 180°C/350°F/Gas Mark 4.
Grease a 19-cm/7½-inch square cake tin and line the
base with baking paper.

STEP 2. Sift together the flour and ginger into a mixing
bowl. In a separate bowl, beat together the eggs,
muscovado sugar, treacle, milk and oil. Make a well in the
dry ingredients and add the liquid mixture, beating well
until smooth.

STEP 3. Pour the mixture into the prepared tin. Bake in
the preheated oven for 25–30 minutes, or until risen
and springy to the touch. Leave to cool in the tin for
5 minutes, then turn out onto a wire rack and leave to
cool completely.

STEP 4. To decorate, mix the icing sugar with the lemon
extract and enough water to make a fairly thick paste.
Drizzle over the cake and sprinkle with the dragées.
Leave to set, then cut into squares.

frosting-topped carrot cake

Serves 12

Difficulty: Medium

Prep: 30 mins, plus cooling and setting
Cook: 40–50 mins

INGREDIENTS

butter, for greasing

2 eggs

175 g/6 oz light muscovado
  sugar

200 ml/7 fl oz sunflower oil

200 g/7 oz carrots, coarsely
  grated

225 g/8 oz plain wholemeal
  flour

1 tsp bicarbonate of soda

2 tsp ground cinnamon

1 tsp ground nutmeg

115 g/4 oz walnuts,
  roughly chopped

FROSTING

115 g/4 oz cream cheese

50 g/1¾ oz unsalted butter,
  softened

85 g/3 oz icing sugar

1 tsp grated lemon rind

1 tsp grated orange rind

STEP 1. Preheat the oven to 190°C/375°F/Gas Mark 5. Grease a 23-cm/9-inch square cake tin and line with baking paper.

STEP 2. Put the eggs into a mixing bowl and beat well, then add the muscovado sugar and oil. Mix well and add the carrot. Sift in the flour, bicarbonate of soda, cinnamon and nutmeg, then add the walnuts. Mix together until all the ingredients are well incorporated.

STEP 3. Spoon the mixture into the prepared tin and smooth the surface with a palette knife. Bake in the preheated oven for 40–50 minutes until the cake is risen and firm to the touch and has begun to shrink away slightly from the side of the tin. Leave to cool in the tin until just warm, then turn out onto a wire rack and leave to cool completely.

STEP 4. To make the frosting, put all the ingredients into a mixing bowl and beat together for 2–3 minutes until smooth. Spread the frosting over the cooled cake, smooth with a fork and leave to firm up a little, then cut the cake into slices.

walnut & banana cake

Serves 12

Difficulty: Easy

Prep: 25 mins, plus cooling

Cook: 1–1¼ hours

INGREDIENTS

250 g/9 oz plain wholemeal flour

1 tsp salt

1 heaped tsp baking powder

1 tsp ground cinnamon

4 ripe bananas

100 ml/3½ fl oz groundnut oil, plus extra for oiling

25 g/1 oz unsalted butter, softened

175 g/6 oz soft light brown sugar

2 large eggs, beaten

175 g/6 oz walnut pieces

STEP 1. Preheat the oven to 180°C/350°F/Gas Mark 4. Lightly oil a 1-kg/2 lb 4-oz loaf tin.

STEP 2. Sift the flour, salt, baking powder and cinnamon into a mixing bowl, tipping in any bran left in the sieve. Stir thoroughly with a fork.

STEP 3. Peel the bananas and mash with a fork. Add to the bowl with the oil, butter, sugar and eggs and beat together until smooth. Fold in the walnuts.

STEP 4. Spoon the mixture into the prepared tin and level the surface. Bake in the preheated oven for 1–1¼ hours, or until a skewer inserted into the centre of the cake comes out clean. Leave to cool in the tin for 5 minutes, then turn out onto a wire rack and leave to cool completely.

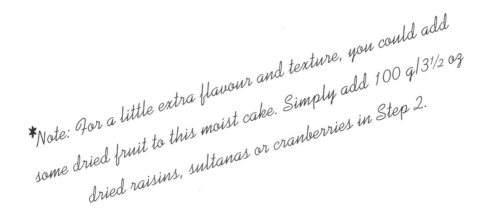

*Note: For a little extra flavour and texture, you could add some dried fruit to this moist cake. Simply add 100 g/3½ oz dried raisins, sultanas or cranberries in Step 2.

cherry & almond cake

Serves 8

Difficulty: Easy

Prep: 30 mins, plus cooling

Cook: 1½–1¾ hours

INGREDIENTS

300 g/10½ oz glacé cherries

175 g/6 oz unsalted butter, softened, plus extra for greasing

175 g/6 oz golden caster sugar

3 eggs

40 g/1½ oz ground almonds

280 g/10 oz plain flour

1½ tsp baking powder

70 g/2½ oz flaked almonds

STEP 1. Preheat the oven to 160°C/325°F/Gas Mark 3. Grease an 18-cm/7-inch square cake tin and line with baking paper.

STEP 2. Cut the cherries in half, then put them in a sieve and rinse to remove all the syrup. Pat dry with kitchen paper and set aside.

STEP 3. Put the butter, sugar, eggs and ground almonds into a mixing bowl. Sift in the flour and baking powder. Beat thoroughly until smooth, then stir in the cherries. Spoon the mixture into the prepared tin and smooth the top. Sprinkle the flaked almonds over the cake mixture.

STEP 4. Bake in the preheated oven for 1½–1¾ hours until well risen and a skewer inserted into the centre of the cake comes out clean.

STEP 5. Leave to cool in the tin for 10 minutes, then turn out onto a wire rack and leave to cool completely.

pear & ginger cake

Serves 8–10

Difficulty: Easy

Prep: 35 mins, plus cooling
Cook: 35–40 mins

INGREDIENTS

200 g/7 oz unsalted butter, softened, plus extra for greasing

200 g/7 oz caster sugar

200 g/7 oz self-raising flour

1 tbsp ground ginger

3 eggs, lightly beaten

450 g/1 lb pears, peeled, cored and thinly sliced

1 tbsp soft light brown sugar

STEP 1. Preheat the oven to 180°C/350°F/Gas Mark 4. Grease a 20-cm/8-inch round cake tin and line with baking paper.

STEP 2. Put 175 g/6 oz of the butter into a mixing bowl with the caster sugar. Sift in the flour and ginger and add the eggs. Beat well until smooth.

STEP 3. Spoon the mixture into the prepared tin and smooth the surface with a palette knife. Arrange the pear slices over the cake mixture. Sprinkle with the brown sugar and dot with the remaining butter.

STEP 4. Bake in the preheated oven for 35–40 minutes, or until the cake is golden and feels springy to the touch.

STEP 5. Leave the cake to cool slightly in the tin, then turn out onto a wire rack and leave to cool completely.

spiced apple & sultana cake

Serves 8–10

Difficulty: Easy

Prep: 35 mins, plus cooling
Cook: 1–1¼ hours

INGREDIENTS

225 g/8 oz unsalted butter, softened, plus extra for greasing

225 g/8 oz light muscovado sugar

4 large eggs, lightly beaten

225 g/8 oz self-raising flour

2 tsp ground cinnamon

½ tsp ground nutmeg

85 g/3 oz sultanas

3 small apples, peeled, cored and thinly sliced

2 tbsp honey, warmed

STEP 1. Preheat the oven to 180°C/350°F/Gas Mark 4. Grease a 23-cm/9-inch round springform cake tin and line with baking paper.

STEP 2. Put the butter and sugar into a mixing bowl and beat together until light and fluffy. Gradually beat in the eggs. Sift the flour, cinnamon and nutmeg into the mixture and gently fold in using a metal spoon. Fold in the sultanas.

STEP 3. Spoon half the mixture into the prepared tin and level the surface. Scatter over half the sliced apples. Spoon over the remaining cake mixture and gently level the surface. Arrange the remaining apple slices over the top.

STEP 4. Bake in the preheated oven for 1–1¼ hours until risen, golden brown and firm to the touch. Leave to cool in the tin for 10 minutes, then turn out onto a wire rack. Brush the top of the cake with the honey and leave to cool completely.

blueberry orange streusel cake

Serves 8–10

Difficulty: Easy

Prep: 25 mins, plus cooling
Cook: 1 hour–1 hour 10 mins

INGREDIENTS

oil or melted butter,
  for greasing

175 g/6 oz plain flour

2 tsp baking powder

175 g/6 oz unsalted butter,
  softened

175 g/6 oz caster sugar

3 eggs, beaten

1 tsp vanilla extract

finely grated rind of
  ½ orange

55 g/2 oz ground almonds

125 g/4½ oz fresh
  blueberries

TOPPING

55 g/2 oz plain flour

25 g/1 oz unsalted butter,
  softened

25 g/1 oz caster sugar

finely grated rind of
  ½ orange

STEP 1. Preheat the oven to 160°C/325°F/Gas Mark 3. Grease a 23-cm/9-inch round springform cake tin and line the base with baking paper.

STEP 2 To make the topping, put all the ingredients into a bowl and stir with a fork to make a crumbly mixture.

STEP 3. Sift the flour and baking powder into a mixing bowl and add the butter, sugar, eggs and vanilla extract. Beat well until smooth, then add the orange rind, ground almonds and half the blueberries.

STEP 4. Spoon the mixture into the prepared tin, smooth the surface with a palette knife and scatter over the remaining blueberries. Sprinkle the topping over the mixture, covering it completely.

STEP 5. Bake in the preheated oven for 1 hour–1 hour 10 minutes, or until risen, firm and golden brown. Leave to cool in the tin for 10 minutes, then unclip and remove the springform and transfer the cake to a wire rack to cool completely.

lemon drizzle loaf

Serves 8–10

Difficulty: Medium

Prep: 30 mins, plus cooling
Cook: 45–55 mins

INGREDIENTS

oil or melted butter,
  for greasing

175 g/6 oz plain flour

1 tbsp baking powder

175 g/6 oz unsalted butter,
  softened

175 g/6 oz golden caster
  sugar

3 eggs, beaten

1 egg yolk

finely grated rind of 1 lemon

2 tbsp lemon juice

fine strips of lemon zest,
  to decorate

SYRUP

85 g/3 oz icing sugar

3 tbsp lemon juice

STEP 1. Preheat the oven to 180°C/350°F/Gas Mark 4. Grease a 1.2-litre/2-pint loaf tin and line with baking paper.

STEP 2. Sift the flour and baking powder into a mixing bowl and add the butter, caster sugar, eggs and egg yolk. Beat well until smooth, then stir in the lemon rind and juice.

STEP 3. Spoon the mixture into the prepared tin and smooth the surface with a palette knife. Bake in the preheated oven for 40–50 minutes, or until well risen, firm and golden brown. Remove from the oven and transfer in the tin to a wire rack.

STEP 4. To make the syrup, put the icing sugar and lemon juice into a saucepan and heat gently without boiling, stirring until the sugar dissolves.

STEP 5. Prick the top of the loaf several times with a skewer and spoon over the syrup. Leave to cool completely in the tin, then turn out, scatter with strips of lemon zest and cut into slices.

clementine cake

Serves 8

Difficulty: Medium

Prep: 35 mins, plus cooling

Cook: 1 hour–1 hour 5 mins

INGREDIENTS

175 g/6 oz unsalted butter, softened, plus extra for greasing

175 g/6 oz caster sugar

grated rind of 2 clementines

3 eggs, beaten

175 g/6 oz self-raising flour

3 tbsp ground almonds

3 tbsp single cream

GLAZE & TOPPING

6 tbsp clementine juice

2 tbsp caster sugar

3 white sugar cubes, crushed

STEP 1. Preheat the oven to 180°C/350°F/Gas Mark 4. Grease an 18-cm/7-inch round cake tin and line the base with baking paper.

STEP 2. Put the butter, sugar and clementine rind into a mixing bowl and cream together until light and fluffy. Gradually add the eggs, beating well after each addition.

STEP 3. Gently fold in the flour, followed by the ground almonds and cream. Spoon the mixture into the prepared tin.

STEP 4. Bake in the preheated oven for 55–60 minutes, or until a skewer inserted into the centre comes out clean. Leave to cool slightly in the tin.

STEP 5. Meanwhile, make the glaze. Put the clementine juice into a small saucepan with the caster sugar. Bring to the boil and simmer for about 5 minutes.

STEP 6. Transfer the cake to a wire rack. Drizzle the glaze over the cake until it has been absorbed and sprinkle with the crushed sugar cubes.

butternut squash & orange cake

Serves 6–8

Difficulty: Medium

Prep: 35–40 mins, plus cooling
Cook: 1 hour

INGREDIENTS

175 g/6 oz unsalted butter,
  softened, plus extra for
  greasing

175 g/6 oz soft light brown
  sugar

3 eggs, beaten

finely grated rind of
  1 orange

225 g/8 oz wholemeal
  self-raising flour

1 tsp baking powder

1 tsp ground cinnamon

225 g/8 oz prepared
  butternut squash flesh,
  coarsely grated

115 g/4 oz sultanas

juice of 1 orange

225 g/8 oz full-fat soft cheese

55 g/2 oz icing sugar, sifted

strips of orange zest,
  to decorate

STEP 1. Preheat the oven to 180°C/350°F/Gas Mark 4. Grease an 18-cm/7-inch round cake tin and line with baking paper.

STEP 2. Put the butter and brown sugar into a mixing bowl and cream together until light and fluffy. Gradually beat in the eggs, beating well after each addition. Reserving 1 teaspoon for the topping, beat the orange rind into the creamed mixture. Fold in the flour, baking powder and cinnamon, then stir in the squash, sultanas and about 1 tablespoon of the orange juice, if necessary, to give a fairly soft consistency. Spoon the mixture into the prepared tin and level the surface.

STEP 3. Bake in the preheated oven for 1 hour, or until risen, firm to the touch and golden brown. Leave to cool in the tin for a few minutes, then turn out onto a wire rack and leave to cool completely.

STEP 4. To make the topping, put the soft cheese, icing sugar, reserved orange rind and 2–3 teaspoons of the remaining orange juice into a bowl and beat together until smooth and combined. Spread over the top of the cooled cake, swirling it attractively, then decorate with strips of orange zest.

small cakes & slices

vanilla-frosted cupcakes

Makes 12

Difficulty: Medium

Prep: 25 mins, plus cooling
Cook: 20 mins

INGREDIENTS

115 g/4 oz butter, softened

115 g/4 oz caster sugar

2 eggs, lightly beaten

115 g/4 oz self-raising flour

1 tbsp milk

1 tbsp hundreds and
  thousands

FROSTING

175 g/6 oz unsalted butter,
  softened

1 tsp vanilla extract

280 g/10 oz icing sugar

STEP 1. Preheat the oven to 180°C/350°F/Gas Mark 4. Line a 12-hole bun tin with paper cases, or put 12 double-layer paper cases on a baking tray.

STEP 2. Put the butter and caster sugar into a mixing bowl and cream together until light and fluffy. Gradually beat in the eggs. Sift in the flour and, using a metal spoon, fold into the mixture with the milk. Spoon the mixture into the paper cases.

STEP 3. Bake the cupcakes in the preheated oven for 20 minutes, or until golden brown and firm to the touch. Transfer to a wire rack and leave to cool.

STEP 4. To make the frosting, put the butter and vanilla extract into a mixing bowl and, beat with a hand-held electric mixer until the butter is pale and very soft. Gradually sift in the icing sugar, beating well after each addition.

STEP 5. When the cupcakes are cold, spoon the frosting into a large piping bag fitted with a medium star-shaped nozzle and pipe a large swirl of frosting on the top of each cupcake. Sprinkle with the hundreds and thousands.

lemon butterfly cupcakes

Makes 12

Difficulty: Medium
Prep: 35 mins, plus cooling
Cook: 15–20 mins

INGREDIENTS

115 g/4 oz self-raising flour

½ tsp baking powder

115 g/4 oz soft margarine

115 g/4 oz caster sugar

2 eggs, lightly beaten

finely grated rind of
 ½ lemon

2 tbsp milk

LEMON FILLING

85 g/3 oz unsalted butter,
 softened

175 g/6 oz icing sugar

1 tbsp lemon juice

STEP 1. Preheat the oven to 190°C/375°F/Gas Mark 5. Line a 12-hole bun tin with paper cases, or put 12 double-layer paper cases on a baking tray.

STEP 2. Sift the flour and baking powder into a mixing bowl. Add the margarine, caster sugar, eggs, lemon rind and milk and beat with a hand-held electric mixer until smooth. Spoon the mixture into the paper cases.

STEP 3. Bake in the preheated oven for 15–20 minutes, or until well risen and golden brown. Transfer to a wire rack and leave to cool.

STEP 4. To make the filling, put the butter into a mixing bowl and beat until fluffy. Sift in the icing sugar, add the lemon juice and beat together until smooth and creamy.

STEP 5. When the cupcakes are cold, use a serrated knife to cut a round from the top of each cupcake, then cut each round in half. Spread or pipe a little of the filling on top of each cupcake, then press the two half-rounds of cake into it at an angle to resemble butterfly wings.

double ginger cupcakes

Makes 12

Difficulty: Easy

Prep: 25 mins, plus cooling
Cook: 15–20 mins

INGREDIENTS

175 g/6 oz plain flour

1 tbsp baking powder

2 tsp ground ginger

175 g/6 oz unsalted butter, softened

175 g/6 oz light muscovado sugar

3 eggs, beaten

25 g/1 oz crystallized stem ginger, finely chopped, plus extra to decorate

FROSTING

200 g/7 oz ricotta cheese

85 g/3 oz icing sugar, sifted

finely grated rind of 1 tangerine

STEP 1. Preheat the oven to 190°C/375°F/Gas Mark 5. Line a 12-hole bun tin with paper cases, or put 12 double-layer paper cases on a baking tray.

STEP 2. Sift the flour, baking powder and ground ginger into a mixing bowl. Add the butter, muscovado sugar and eggs and beat well until smooth. Stir in the crystallized ginger. Spoon the mixture into the paper cases.

STEP 3. Bake in the preheated oven for 15–20 minutes until well risen. Transfer to a wire rack and leave to cool.

STEP 4. To make the frosting, put the ricotta cheese, icing sugar and tangerine rind into a mixing bowl and mix together until smooth.

STEP 5. Spoon a little frosting onto each cupcake and spread to cover the top completely. Decorate with crystallized ginger.

chocolate hazelnut cupcakes

Makes 18

Difficulty: Easy

Prep: 15 mins, plus cooling
Cook: 20–25 mins

INGREDIENTS

175 g/6 oz unsalted butter, softened

115 g/4 oz soft light brown sugar

2 large eggs, lightly beaten

2 tbsp chocolate hazelnut spread

175 g/6 oz self-raising flour

50 g/1¾ oz blanched hazelnuts, coarsely ground

TOPPING

5 tbsp chocolate hazelnut spread

18 whole blanched hazelnuts

STEP 1. Preheat the oven to 180°C/350°F/Gas Mark 4. Line two 9-hole bun tins with paper cases, or put 18 double-layer paper cases on a large baking tray.

STEP 2. Put the butter and sugar into a mixing bowl and cream together until light and fluffy. Gradually beat in the eggs, then stir in the chocolate hazelnut spread. Sift in the flour and fold into the mixture with the ground hazelnuts. Spoon the mixture into the paper cases.

STEP 3. Bake in the preheated oven for 20–25 minutes, or until risen and firm to the touch. Transfer to a wire rack and leave to cool completely.

STEP 4. Swirl some chocolate hazelnut spread over the top of each cooled cupcake and top with a hazelnut.

*Note: Chocolate hazelnut spread is a really versatile storecupboard ingredient — spread it on toast, sandwich cookies together with a generous layer or use it in your baking, as here.

jam doughnut muffins

Makes 12

Difficulty: Medium

Prep: 20 mins, plus 5 mins cooling
Cook: 20 mins

INGREDIENTS

oil or melted butter,
  for greasing

280 g/10 oz plain flour

1 tbsp baking powder

⅛ tsp salt

115 g/4 oz caster sugar

2 eggs

200 ml/7 fl oz milk

6 tbsp sunflower oil or 85 g/
  3 oz unsalted butter, melted
  and cooled

1 tsp vanilla extract

12 tsp raspberry jam or
  strawberry jam

TOPPING

150 g/5½ oz granulated
  sugar

115 g/4 oz butter, melted

STEP 1. Preheat the oven to 200°C/400°F/Gas Mark 6. Grease a 12-hole muffin tin.

STEP 2. Sift together the flour, baking powder and salt into a mixing bowl. Stir in the caster sugar.

STEP 3. Lightly beat the eggs in a large jug or bowl, then beat in the milk, oil and vanilla extract. Make a well in the centre of the dry ingredients and pour in the beaten liquid ingredients. Stir gently until just combined; do not over-mix.

STEP 4. Spoon half of the mixture into the prepared muffin tin. Add a teaspoon of jam to the centre of each, then spoon in the remaining mixture. Bake in the preheated oven for about 20 minutes, or until well risen, golden brown and firm to the touch. Leave to cool in the tin for 5 minutes.

STEP 5. Meanwhile, prepare the topping. Spread out the sugar on a wide plate. Dip the tops of the muffins in the melted butter, then roll in the sugar. Serve warm or transfer to a wire rack and leave to cool.

blueberry bran muffins

Makes 10

Difficulty: Easy

Prep: 20 mins, plus cooling
Cook: 20 mins

INGREDIENTS

150 g/5½ oz white plain flour

100 g/3½ oz light brown
  self-raising flour

1 tbsp oat bran

2 tsp baking powder

½ tsp bicarbonate of soda

pinch of salt

50 g/1¼ oz demerara sugar

1 tbsp honey

1 large egg

200 ml/7 fl oz buttermilk

150 g/5½ oz fresh
  blueberries

STEP 1. Preheat the oven to 180°C/350°F/Gas Mark 4. Line a muffin tin with 10 paper cases, or put 10 double-layer paper cases on a baking tray.

STEP 2. Put the white flour, brown flour, bran, baking powder, bicarbonate of soda and salt into a mixing bowl, mix well together and stir in the sugar. Whisk together the honey, egg and buttermilk in a jug.

STEP 3. Pour the wet ingredients into the dry mixture and gently stir until just combined; do not over-mix. Fold in the blueberries.

STEP 4. Spoon the mixture into the paper cases. Bake in the preheated oven for 20 minutes until the muffins are risen and light brown. Transfer to a wire rack and leave to cool completely.

lemon & poppy seed muffins

Makes 12

Difficulty: Easy

Prep: 30 mins, plus cooling
Cook: 45 mins

INGREDIENTS

280 g/10 oz plain flour

1 tbsp baking powder

⅛ tsp salt

115 g/4 oz caster sugar

2 tbsp poppy seeds

2 eggs

250 ml/9 fl oz milk

6 tbsp sunflower oil or
  85 g/3 oz unsalted butter,
  melted and cooled

finely grated rind of
  2 lemons

STEP 1. Preheat the oven to 200°C/400°F/Gas Mark 6. Line a 12-hole muffin tin with paper cases, or put 12 double-layer paper cases on a baking tray.

STEP 2. Sift together the flour, baking powder and salt into a mixing bowl. Stir in the sugar and poppy seeds.

STEP 3. Lightly beat the eggs in a large jug or bowl, then beat in the milk, oil and lemon rind. Make a well in the centre of the dry ingredients and pour in the beaten liquid ingredients. Stir gently until just combined; do not over-mix.

STEP 4. Spoon the mixture into the paper cases. Bake in the preheated oven for about 20 minutes until well risen, golden brown and firm to the touch.

STEP 5. Remove the muffins from the oven, transfer to a wire rack and leave to cool.

*Note: Muffins are incredibly easy to make, but you must take care not to over-mix the batter — it's best to have some flour showing when the muffins go into the oven.

coconut lamingtons

Makes 16

Difficulty: Hard

Prep: 30 mins, plus cooling and setting
Cook: 30–35 mins

INGREDIENTS

oil or melted butter,
  for greasing

175 g/6 oz plain flour

1 tbsp baking powder

175 g/6 oz unsalted butter,
  softened

175 g/6 oz caster sugar

3 eggs, beaten

1 tsp vanilla extract

2 tbsp milk

2 tbsp desiccated coconut

FROSTING

500 g/1 lb 2 oz icing sugar

40 g/1½ oz cocoa powder

85 ml/3 fl oz boiling water

70 g/2½ oz unsalted butter,
  melted

250 g/9 oz desiccated
  coconut

STEP 1. Preheat the oven to 180°C/350°F/Gas Mark 4. Grease a 23-cm/9-inch square cake tin and line with baking paper.

STEP 2. Sift the flour and baking powder into a mixing bowl and add the butter, caster sugar, eggs and vanilla extract. Beat well until smooth, then stir in the milk and coconut.

STEP 3. Spoon the mixture into the prepared tin and smooth the surface with a palette knife. Bake in the preheated oven for 30–35 minutes, or until risen, firm and golden brown.

STEP 4. Leave to cool in the tin for 10 minutes, then turn out onto a wire rack and leave to cool completely. Cut the cooled cake into 16 squares with a sharp knife.

STEP 5. To make the frosting, sift the icing sugar and cocoa powder into a bowl. Add the water and butter and stir until smooth. Spread out the coconut on a large plate. Dip each piece of cake into the frosting, holding it with two forks to coat evenly, then toss in the coconut until coated on all sides. Place on a sheet of baking paper and leave to set.

chocolate madeleines

Makes 30

Difficulty: Medium

Prep: 20 mins, plus cooling
Cook: 8–10 mins

INGREDIENTS

3 eggs

1 egg yolk

1 tsp vanilla extract

140 g/5 oz caster sugar

115 g/4 oz plain flour

25 g/1 oz cocoa powder

1 tsp baking powder

140 g/5 oz unsalted butter,
   melted and cooled, plus
   extra for greasing

icing sugar, for dusting

STEP 1. Preheat the oven to 190°C/375°F/Gas Mark 5. Lightly grease 30 holes in two or three standard-sized madeleine tins.

STEP 2. Put the eggs, egg yolk, vanilla extract and caster sugar into a mixing bowl and beat with a hand-held electric mixer until very pale and thick.

STEP 3. Sift in the flour, cocoa powder and baking powder and fold in lightly and evenly using a metal spoon. Fold in the melted butter evenly.

STEP 4. Spoon the mixture into the prepared tins, filling the holes to about three-quarters full. Bake in the preheated oven for 8–10 minutes until risen and springy to the touch.

STEP 5. Carefully remove the cakes from the tins and transfer to a wire rack to cool. Lightly dust with icing sugar before serving.

*Note: These deliciously light shell-shaped cakes don't store well and are best eaten on the day they are made.

cherry & sultana scones

Makes 8

Difficulty: Medium

Prep: 30 mins, plus cooling
Cook: 8–10 mins

INGREDIENTS

225 g/8 oz self-raising flour,
  plus extra for dusting

1 tbsp caster sugar

pinch of salt

85 g/3 oz unsalted butter,
  cut into small pieces, plus
  extra for greasing

3 tbsp glacé cherries,
  chopped

3 tbsp sultanas

1 egg, lightly beaten

3 tbsp milk

STEP 1. Preheat the oven to 220°C/425°F/Gas Mark 7. Grease a baking tray and line with baking paper.

STEP 2. Sift the flour, sugar and salt into a mixing bowl and rub in the butter with your fingertips until the mixture resembles breadcrumbs.

STEP 3. Stir in the glacé cherries and sultanas. Add the egg and 2 tablespoons of the milk. Mix well together to form a soft dough.

STEP 4. Turn out the dough onto a lightly floured work surface and roll out to a thickness of 2 cm/¾ inch. Cut out eight rounds using a 5-cm/2-inch biscuit cutter.

STEP 5. Place the scones on the prepared tray and brush the tops with the remaining milk.

STEP 6. Bake in the preheated oven for 8–10 minutes, or until golden brown. Transfer to a wire rack and leave to cool completely.

rock cakes

Makes 8

Difficulty: Easy

Prep: 20 mins, plus cooling
Cook: 15–20 mins

INGREDIENTS

225 g/8 oz plain flour

2 tsp baking powder

115 g/4 oz unsalted butter,
   plus extra for greasing

85 g/3 oz soft light brown
   sugar

85 g/3 oz mixed dried fruit

finely grated rind of 1 lemon

1 egg

1–2 tbsp milk

2 tsp demerara sugar

STEP 1. Preheat the oven to 200°C/400°F/Gas Mark 6. Lightly grease two baking trays.

STEP 2. Sift the flour and baking powder into a mixing bowl. Add the butter and rub it in with your fingertips until the mixture resembles breadcrumbs. Stir in the brown sugar, mixed dried fruit and lemon rind.

STEP 3. Put the egg and 1 tablespoon of the milk into a small bowl and lightly beat, then stir into the flour mixture, adding a little more milk if necessary, until it starts to bind together to form a moist but firm dough. Spoon eight heaps of the mixture onto the prepared trays and sprinkle with the demerara sugar.

STEP 4. Bake in the preheated oven for 15–20 minutes, or until golden brown and firm. Use a palette knife to transfer the cakes to a wire rack and leave to cool.

*Note: Do not be tempted to smooth the heaps of batter before putting the trays in the oven — these are called rock cakes because of their characteristically rugged appearance.

apple turnovers

Makes 8

Difficulty: Medium

Prep: 40 mins, plus cooling
Cook: 15–20 mins

INGREDIENTS

250 g/9 oz ready-made puff
  pastry

plain flour, for dusting

milk, for glazing

FILLING

450 g/1 lb cooking apples,
  peeled, cored and chopped

grated rind of 1 lemon
  (optional)

pinch of ground cloves
  (optional)

3 tbsp granulated sugar

ORANGE SUGAR

1 tbsp granulated sugar

finely grated rind of
  1 orange

ORANGE CREAM

250 ml/9 fl oz double cream

grated rind of 1 orange

juice of ½ orange

icing sugar, to taste

STEP 1. To make the filling, mix together the apples, lemon rind and ground cloves, if using, but do not add the sugar until the last minute. To make the orange sugar, mix together the sugar and orange rind.

STEP 2. Preheat the oven to 220°C/425°F/Gas Mark 7. Roll out the pastry on a floured work surface to a 60 x 30-cm/24 x 12-inch rectangle. Cut the rectangle in half lengthways, then cut it across four times to make eight 15-cm/6-inch squares.

STEP 3. Mix the granulated sugar into the apple filling. Lightly brush each pastry square with milk and place a little of the apple filling in the centre. Fold over a corner diagonally to meet the opposite corner, making a triangle, and press the edges together very firmly. Place on a baking tray. Repeat with the remaining squares.

STEP 4. Brush the turnovers with milk and sprinkle with the orange sugar. Bake in the preheated oven for 15–20 minutes until puffed and well browned. Transfer to a wire rack to cool slightly.

STEP 5. Meanwhile, to make the orange cream, whip the cream with the orange rind and orange juice until thick. Add icing sugar to taste and whip again until soft peaks hold. Serve the turnovers warm with the orange cream.

double chocolate swirls

Makes 24

Difficulty: Medium

Prep: 40 mins, plus cooling and 1½–2 hours standing
Cook: 15–20 mins

INGREDIENTS

600 g/1 lb 5 oz strong white
  flour, plus extra for dusting

7 g/¼ oz easy-blend
  dried yeast

115 g/4 oz caster sugar

½ tsp salt

1 tsp ground cinnamon

85 g/3 oz unsalted butter

2 large eggs, beaten, plus
  extra for glazing

300 ml/10 fl oz milk

oil, for greasing

FILLING

6 tbsp chocolate hazelnut
  spread

200 g/7 oz milk chocolate,
  chopped

STEP 1. Put the flour, yeast, sugar, salt and cinnamon into a mixing bowl and mix together.

STEP 2. Melt the butter in a heatproof bowl set over a saucepan of gently simmering water, then leave to cool slightly. Whisk in the eggs and milk. Pour into the flour mixture and mix well until a dough forms.

STEP 3. Turn out the dough onto a floured work surface and knead for 10 minutes until smooth. Put into a large floured bowl, cover with clingfilm and leave to stand in a warm place for 1½–2 hours.

STEP 4. When you are ready to make the buns, take the dough from the bowl and knock back. Preheat the oven to 220°C/425°F/Gas Mark 7. Lightly oil two baking trays.

STEP 5. Divide the dough into four pieces and roll out each piece to a 2.5-cm/1-inch thick rectangle. Spread each rectangle with some of the chocolate hazelnut spread and scatter over a little chopped chocolate. Roll up each piece from one of the long edges, then cut into six pieces. Place each swirl cut side down on one of the prepared trays and brush with the beaten egg. Bake in the preheated oven for 12–15 minutes until golden brown. Serve warm.

raspberry chocolate éclairs

Makes about 12

Difficulty: Hard

Prep: 30 mins, plus cooling and setting
Cook: 40–45 mins

INGREDIENTS

CHOUX PASTRY

55 g/2 oz butter

150 ml/5 fl oz water

70 g/2½ oz plain flour, sifted

2 eggs, beaten

FILLING & TOPPING

175 ml/6 fl oz double cream

1 tbsp icing sugar

175 g/6 oz fresh raspberries

85 g/3 oz plain chocolate,
  broken into pieces

STEP 1. Preheat the oven to 220°C/425°F/Gas Mark 7. Dampen a baking tray with water.

STEP 2. To make the choux pastry, put the butter and water into a heavy-based saucepan and bring to the boil over a low heat. Add the flour, all at once, and beat thoroughly until the mixture leaves the side of the pan. Leave to cool slightly, then vigorously beat in the eggs, a little at a time.

STEP 3. Spoon the mixture into a piping bag fitted with a 1-cm/½-inch plain nozzle and pipe 7.5-cm/3-inch lengths onto the prepared tray. Bake in the preheated oven for 10 minutes, then reduce the oven temperature to 190°C/375°F/Gas Mark 5 and bake for an additional 20 minutes, or until crisp and golden brown. Split the side of each éclair to let the steam escape, then transfer to a wire rack to cool completely.

STEP 4. To make the filling, put the cream and icing sugar into a bowl and whip until thick. Split the éclairs lengthways and spoon in the cream mixture. Place a few raspberries in each éclair.

STEP 5. Put the chocolate into a heatproof bowl set over a saucepan of gently simmering water and heat until melted. Spread a little on top of each éclair. Leave to set, then serve.

chocolate nut brownies

Makes 16

Difficulty: Easy

Prep: 20 mins, plus cooling
Cook: 35 mins

INGREDIENTS

groundnut oil, for oiling

225 g/8 oz plain chocolate

175 g/6 oz soft margarine

3 large eggs

100 g/3½ oz caster sugar

175 g/6 oz self-raising flour

100 g/3½ oz walnuts or
  blanched hazelnuts,
  chopped

50 g/1¾ oz milk chocolate
  chips

STEP 1. Preheat the oven to 180°C/350°F/Gas Mark 4. Lightly oil a 25-cm/10-inch square cake tin.

STEP 2. Put the chocolate and margarine into a heatproof bowl set over a saucepan of gently simmering water and heat until melted. Remove the bowl from the pan and stir well to combine the chocolate and margarine.

STEP 3. Meanwhile, put the eggs and sugar together into a mixing bowl and beat until pale and creamy. Stir in the melted chocolate mixture, then add the flour, walnuts and chocolate chips. Mix together well.

STEP 4. Spoon the mixture into the prepared tin. Bake in the preheated oven for 30 minutes, or until the top is set and the centre is still slightly sticky. Leave to cool in the tin, then lift out and cut into squares.

chocolate chip & walnut slices

Makes 18

Difficulty: Easy

Prep: 20 mins, plus cooling
Cook: 20–25 mins

INGREDIENTS

115 g/4 oz walnut pieces

225 g/8 oz unsalted butter,
   plus extra for greasing

175 g/6 oz caster sugar

a few drops of vanilla extract

225 g/8 oz plain flour

200 g/7 oz plain chocolate
   chips

STEP 1. Preheat the oven to 180°C/350°F/Gas Mark 4. Grease a 20 x 30-cm/8 x 12-inch Swiss roll tin and line with baking paper.

STEP 2. Roughly chop the walnut pieces to about the same size as the chocolate chips and set aside.

STEP 3. Put the butter and sugar into a mixing bowl and cream together until light and fluffy. Add the vanilla extract, then stir in the flour. Stir in the reserved walnuts and the chocolate chips. Press the mixture into the prepared tin.

STEP 4. Bake in the preheated oven for 20–25 minutes until golden. Leave to cool in the tin, then cut into slices.

*Note: You can make these luscious slices with any type of nut – try hazelnuts for a perfect flavour combination, or pistachio nuts for a colour contrast.

coconut paradise slices

Makes 16

Difficulty: Medium

Prep: 30 mins, plus 1 hour setting, and cooling
Cook: 45 mins

INGREDIENTS

200 g/7 oz plain chocolate, broken into pieces

100 g/3½ oz unsalted butter, plus extra for greasing

200 g/7 oz caster sugar

2 large eggs, lightly beaten

200 g/7 oz desiccated coconut

100 g/3½ oz sultanas

100 g/3½ oz glacé cherries

STEP 1. Grease a 23-cm/9-inch square cake tin and line with baking paper. Put the chocolate into a heatproof bowl set over a saucepan of gently simmering water and heat until melted. Remove from the heat and stir until smooth. Pour into the prepared tin and leave to set for about 1 hour.

STEP 2. Preheat the oven to 180°C/350°F/Gas Mark 4. Put the butter and sugar into a mixing bowl and cream together until light and fluffy. Gradually beat in the eggs, then add the coconut, sultanas and glacé cherries and stir to combine. Spoon the mixture over the chocolate in the tin and spread out evenly.

STEP 3. Bake in the preheated oven for 30–35 minutes, or until golden brown. Leave to cool in the tin, then turn out and cut into slices.

*Note: These deliciously moist slices would make an excellent contribution to afternoon tea. You could also include them in a packed lunch as a special treat.

date & nut crumble bars

Makes 12

Difficulty: Easy

Prep: 20 mins, plus cooling
Cook: 40–45 mins

INGREDIENTS

250 g/9 oz unsalted butter,
  plus extra for greasing

225 g/8 oz plain flour

200 g/7 oz porridge oats

175 g/6 oz light muscovado
  sugar

finely grated rind and juice
  of 1 lemon

100 g/3½ oz chopped mixed
  nuts

250 g/9 oz ready-to-eat
  stoned dates, chopped

½ tsp mixed spice

STEP 1. Preheat the oven to 190°C/375°F/Gas Mark 5. Lightly grease a 31 x 17-cm/12½ x 6½-inch cake tin.

STEP 2. Put the butter into a mixing bowl with the flour and oats, then rub in the butter with your fingertips to make coarse crumbs. Stir in 150 g/5½ oz of the sugar, all of the lemon rind and half the chopped nuts, mixing to a crumbly dough.

STEP 3. Tip about two thirds of the mixture into the prepared tin and press with your knuckles to spread evenly over the base. Mix the remaining dough with the remaining nuts, stirring to make a crumbly mixture.

STEP 4. Put the dates into a small saucepan with the remaining sugar, the lemon juice and the mixed spice. Stir until boiling, then simmer for 1–2 minutes, until most of the juices are absorbed. Spread the hot mixture over the dough in the tin, then top with the crumble mixture, pressing down lightly.

STEP 5. Bake in the preheated oven for 35–40 minutes, until golden brown. Leave to cool for about 30 minutes, then cut into bars and leave to cool completely in the tin.

orange flapjack fingers

Makes 18

Difficulty: Easy

Prep: 20 mins, plus cooling
Cook: 30–35

INGREDIENTS

175 g/6 oz unsalted butter,
   plus extra for greasing

150 g/5½ oz golden syrup

70 g/2½ oz demerara sugar

200 g/7 oz porridge oats

70 g/2½ oz plain wholemeal
   flour

70 g/2½ oz raisins or sultanas

finely grated rind of 1 large
   orange

STEP 1. Preheat the oven to 180°C/350°F/Gas Mark 4. Grease a 25 x 20-cm/10 x 8-inch baking tin and line with baking paper.

STEP 2. Put the butter, golden syrup and sugar into a saucepan over a high heat and stir until the butter and syrup have melted and the sugar has dissolved, then bring to the boil without stirring.

STEP 3. Put the oats, flour, raisins and orange rind into a large mixing bowl. Pour in the butter mixture and stir all the ingredients together. Tip into the prepared tin and use the back of a wooden spoon to spread it evenly over the base of the tin and into the corners.

STEP 4. Bake in the preheated oven for 25–30 minutes until set. Leave to cool completely in the tin.

STEP 5. When cool, invert the tin onto a chopping board. Using a serrated knife, cut the flapjack in half lengthways, then cut each half into thick fingers.

cranberry & pecan slices

Makes 12

Difficulty: Easy

Prep: 20 mins, plus cooling
Cook: 35 mins

INGREDIENTS

unsalted butter, for greasing

250 g/9 oz no-added-sugar muesli

75 g/2¾ oz dried cranberries

50 g/1¾ oz pecan nuts, chopped

100 g/3½ oz demerara sugar

3 tbsp clear honey

2 egg whites, lightly beaten

175 ml/6 fl oz apple juice

STEP 1. Preheat the oven to 180°C/350°F/Gas Mark 4. Grease a 22-cm/8½-inch square cake tin and line with baking paper.

STEP 2. Put the muesli, cranberries, pecan nuts and sugar into a mixing bowl and stir to combine.

STEP 3. Heat the honey in a saucepan over a low heat until warm, then stir into the muesli mixture. Stir in the egg whites and apple juice and mix well.

STEP 4. Spoon the mixture into the prepared tin and press down firmly. Bake in the preheated oven for 30 minutes until golden brown. Leave to cool in the tin, then cut into 12 slices.

*Note: These chewy, colourful slices are a good choice for a lunchbox treat, but they're also a delicious accompaniment to morning coffee or afternoon tea.

cookies

double chocolate cookies

Makes about 30

Difficulty: Easy

Prep: 25 mins, plus cooling
Cook: 12–15 minutes

INGREDIENTS

225 g/8 oz unsalted butter,
  softened

140 g/5 oz caster sugar

1 egg yolk, lightly beaten

2 tsp vanilla extract

250 g/9 oz plain flour

25 g/1 oz cocoa powder

pinch of salt

350 g/12 oz plain chocolate,
  chopped

55 g/2 oz dried cherries

STEP 1. Preheat the oven to 190°C/375°F/Gas Mark 5. Line two large baking trays with baking paper.

STEP 2. Put the butter and sugar into a mixing bowl and cream together until light and fluffy, then beat in the egg yolk and vanilla extract. Sift the flour, cocoa powder and salt into the mixture, then add the chocolate and cherries and stir until combined.

STEP 3. Scoop up tablespoons of the mixture and shape into balls. Place them on the prepared trays, spaced well apart, and flatten slightly.

STEP 4. Bake in the preheated oven for 12–15 minutes. Leave to cool on the baking trays for 5–10 minutes, then transfer the cookies to wire racks to cool completely.

*Note: The dried cherries provide good colour and flavour contrast to the rich chocolate in these cookies – you could also use dried cranberries, which have a little more tartness.

chewy oat biscuits

Makes 24

Difficulty: Easy

Prep: 20 mins, plus cooling
Cook: 12–14 mins

INGREDIENTS

125 g/4½ oz unsalted butter,
   softened

200 g/7 oz caster sugar

1 large egg

¼ tsp vanilla extract

115 g/4 oz plain white flour

115 g/4 oz plain wholemeal
   flour

¾ tsp bicarbonate of soda

pinch of salt

40 g/1½ oz porridge oats

100 g/3½ oz raisins or
   sultanas

STEP 1. Preheat the oven to 180°C/350°F/Gas Mark 4.

STEP 2. Put the butter and sugar into a mixing bowl and cream together until light and fluffy. Beat in the egg and vanilla extract. Sift in the white flour, wholemeal flour, bicarbonate of soda and salt, tipping in any bran left in the sieve. Add the oats and raisins and stir well.

STEP 3. Shape the dough into 24 equal-sized balls. Place them on baking trays, spaced well apart.

STEP 4. Bake in the preheated oven for 12–14 minutes until golden brown at the edges. Transfer to a wire rack and leave to cool.

*Note: These cookies are an excellent choice for beating that mid-morning sugar dip — the raisins provide natural sweetness and the oats will give you some slow-release energy to help get you through until lunchtime — as an added bonus, they're delicious!

crunchy peanut biscuits

Makes 20

Difficulty: Easy

Prep: 30 mins, plus 30 mins chilling, and cooling
Cook: 15 mins

INGREDIENTS

125 g/4½ oz unsalted butter, softened, plus extra for greasing

150 g/5½ oz chunky peanut butter

225 g/8 oz granulated sugar

1 egg, lightly beaten

150 g/5½ oz plain flour

½ tsp baking powder

pinch of salt

75 g/2¾ oz unsalted peanuts, chopped

STEP 1. Lightly grease two large baking trays.

STEP 2. Put the butter and peanut butter into a mixing bowl and beat together. Gradually add the sugar and beat together well. Add the egg, a little at a time, beating well after each addition, until combined.

STEP 3. Sift the flour, baking powder and salt into the peanut butter mixture. Add the peanuts and bring all of the ingredients together into a soft dough. Wrap the dough in clingfilm and chill in the refrigerator for 30 minutes.

STEP 4. Preheat the oven to 190°C/375°F/Gas Mark 5. Shape the dough into 20 equal-sized balls and place them on the prepared baking trays, about 5 cm/2 inches apart. Flatten them slightly with your hand.

STEP 5. Bake in the preheated oven for 15 minutes until golden brown. Transfer to wire racks and leave to cool.

coconut & cranberry cookies

Makes about 30

Difficulty: Easy

Prep: 20 mins, plus cooling
Cook: 12–15 mins

INGREDIENTS

225 g/8 oz unsalted butter, softened

140 g/5 oz caster sugar

1 egg yolk, lightly beaten

2 tsp vanilla extract

280 g/10 oz plain flour

pinch of salt

40 g/1½ oz desiccated coconut

60 g/2½ oz dried cranberries

STEP 1. Preheat the oven to 190°C/375°F/Gas Mark 5. Line two large baking trays with baking paper.

STEP 2. Put the butter and sugar into a mixing bowl and cream together until light and fluffy, then beat in the egg yolk and vanilla extract. Sift together the flour and salt into the mixture, then add the coconut and cranberries and stir until combined.

STEP 3. Scoop up tablespoons of the dough and place mounds on the prepared baking trays, spaced well apart.

STEP 4. Bake in the preheated oven for 12–15 minutes, or until golden brown. Leave to cool on the baking trays for 5–10 minutes, then transfer to wire racks and leave to cool completely.

lemon chocolate pinwheels

Makes 40

Difficulty: Medium

Prep: 30–35 mins, plus 1 hour chilling, and cooling
Cook: 15–20 mins

INGREDIENTS

175 g/6 oz unsalted butter, softened, plus extra for greasing

250 g/9 oz caster sugar

1 egg, beaten

350 g/12 oz plain flour, plus extra for dusting

25 g/1 oz plain chocolate, broken into pieces

grated rind of 1 lemon

STEP 1. Grease several baking trays and dust with flour, shaking out any excess.

STEP 2. Put the butter and sugar into a mixing bowl and cream together until light and fluffy. Gradually add the egg, beating well after each addition. Sift in the flour and mix thoroughly to a soft dough.

STEP 3. Transfer half the dough to a separate bowl. Put the chocolate into a heatproof bowl set over a saucepan of gently simmering water and heat until melted. Leave to cool slightly. Beat into one half of the dough. Stir the lemon rind into the remaining dough.

STEP 4. Turn out the two doughs onto a lightly floured work surface and roll out to two equal-sized rectangles. Lay the lemon dough on top of the chocolate dough. Roll up tightly, using a sheet of baking paper to guide you. Chill in the refrigerator for 1 hour.

STEP 5. Preheat the oven to 190°C/375°F/Gas Mark 5. Cut the roll into 40 slices, place on the prepared trays and bake in the preheated oven for 10–12 minutes, or until lightly golden. Transfer to a wire rack and leave to cool completely.

crunchy seed & spice cookies

Makes about 22

Difficulty: Easy

Prep: 25 mins, plus cooling
Cook: 12–15 mins

INGREDIENTS

85 g/3 oz unsalted butter,
    plus extra for greasing

85 g/3 oz light muscovado
    sugar

1 egg, beaten

225 g/8 oz plain flour

1 tsp caraway seeds

1 tsp ground nutmeg

55 g/2 oz sunflower seeds

STEP 1. Preheat the oven to 200°C/400°F/Gas Mark 6. Lightly grease two baking trays.

STEP 2. Put the butter and sugar into a mixing bowl and cream together until light and fluffy. Add the egg and beat thoroughly, then stir in the flour, caraway seeds and nutmeg, mixing evenly to a fairly stiff dough.

STEP 3. Roll walnut-sized pieces of dough into balls with your hands. Toss them roughly in the sunflower seeds to coat lightly, then place on the prepared trays and lightly press with your fingers to flatten slightly.

STEP 4. Bake in the preheated oven for 12–15 minutes, or until golden brown. Transfer to a wire rack to cool.

*Note: Keep an eye on the cookies while they are baking — if the sunflower seeds start to brown, cover the trays with foil for the remainder of the cooking time.

thumbprint cookies

Makes about 36

Difficulty: Medium

Prep: 25 mins, plus cooling
Cook: 20–22 minutes

INGREDIENTS

115 g/4 oz unsalted butter,
  softened

125 g/4½ oz caster sugar

1 large egg, separated

1 tsp vanilla extract

175 g/6 oz plain flour

pinch of salt

25 g/1 oz ground almonds

100 g/3½ oz raspberry jam

STEP 1. Preheat the oven to 180°C/350°F/Gas Mark 4. Line two large baking trays with baking paper.

STEP 2. Put the butter and 100 g/3½ oz of the sugar into a mixing bowl and cream together until light and fluffy. Add the egg yolk and vanilla extract and beat well to combine. Sift in the flour and salt and mix well.

STEP 3. Mix the remaining sugar and the ground almonds together and spread out on a plate. Lightly whisk the egg white in a separate bowl. Roll walnut-sized pieces of dough into balls with your hands, then dip each ball into the egg white and roll in the almond sugar. Place the balls on the prepared trays and make a deep indentation in each cookie with your thumb.

STEP 4. Bake in the preheated oven for 10 minutes, then remove from the oven, press down again on each indentation and fill it with a little of the jam. Return to the oven and bake for a further 10–12 minutes, or until golden brown, turning the trays once. Transfer to wire racks and leave to cool completely.

cherry & chocolate diamonds

Makes about 30

Difficulty: Easy

Prep: 25 mins, plus 30 mins–1 hour chilling, and cooling
Cook: 10–15 mins

INGREDIENTS

225 g/8 oz unsalted butter,
  softened

140 g/5 oz caster sugar

1 egg yolk, lightly beaten

2 tsp vanilla extract

280 g/10 oz plain flour

pinch of salt

55 g/2 oz glacé cherries,
  finely chopped

55 g/2 oz milk chocolate
  chips

STEP 1. Put the butter and sugar into a mixing bowl and cream together until light and fluffy, then beat in the egg yolk and vanilla extract. Sift together the flour and salt into the mixture, add the glacé cherries and chocolate chips and stir until thoroughly combined. Halve the dough and shape into two balls, then wrap in clingfilm and chill in the refrigerator for 30 minutes–1 hour.

STEP 2. Preheat the oven to 190°C/375°F/Gas Mark 5. Line two large baking trays with baking paper.

STEP 3. Unwrap the dough and roll out between two sheets of baking paper to a thickness of 3 mm/⅛ inch. Cut out cookies with a diamond-shaped cutter and place them on the prepared trays.

STEP 4. Bake in the preheated oven for 10–15 minutes, or until light golden brown. Leave to cool on the baking trays for 5–10 minutes, then transfer the cookies to wire racks to cool completely.

tangy lemon jumbles

Makes 40

Difficulty: Easy

Prep: 20 mins, plus cooling
Cook: 15–20 mins

INGREDIENTS

groundnut oil, for oiling

100 g/3½ oz unsalted butter, softened

125 g/4½ oz caster sugar

finely grated rind of 1 lemon

1 large egg, lightly beaten

4 tbsp lemon juice

350 g/12 oz plain flour, plus extra for dusting

1 tsp baking powder

1 tbsp milk

STEP 1. Preheat the oven to 160°C/325°F/Gas Mark 3. Oil two large baking trays.

STEP 2. Put the butter, sugar and lemon rind into a mixing bowl and cream together until light and fluffy. Alternately add the egg and lemon juice to the mixture, beating well between each addition. Sift in the flour and baking powder and mix well, then add the milk and mix to a smooth dough.

STEP 3. Turn out the dough onto a floured work surface and divide into 40 equal-sized pieces. Roll each piece into a sausage, then form into an S-shape and place on the prepared trays. Bake in the preheated oven for 15–20 minutes. Transfer to a wire rack to cool.

*Note: These plain-looking cookies have an unexpectedly tangy lemon flavour that bursts in your mouth as soon as you bite into them — if you prefer orange, replace the lemon rind and juice with orange rind and juice.

jam sandwich biscuits

Makes 24

Difficulty: Easy

Prep: 30 mins, plus 2 hours chilling, and cooling
Cook: 25–30 mins

INGREDIENTS

225 g/8 oz unsalted butter,
  softened

100 g/3½ oz caster sugar

200 g/7 oz plain flour,
  plus extra for dusting

pinch of salt

100 g/3½ oz ground almonds

55 g/2 oz raspberry jam

55 g/2 oz apricot jam

2 tbsp icing sugar

STEP 1. Put the butter and caster sugar into a mixing bowl and cream together until light and fluffy. Add the flour, salt and ground almonds and bring together to a soft dough. Wrap the dough in clingfilm and chill in the refrigerator for 2 hours.

STEP 2. Preheat the oven to 150°C/300°F/Gas Mark 2.

STEP 3. Roll out the dough on a floured work surface to a thickness of 5 mm/¼ inch. Using a 7-cm/2¾-inch biscuit cutter dipped in flour, cut out 48 rounds. Use a small round biscuit cutter to cut out the centres from 24 of the rounds, then place the biscuits on two large baking trays. Bake in the preheated oven for 25–30 minutes, or until golden. Transfer to a wire rack to cool completely.

STEP 4. Spoon the raspberry jam onto 12 of the complete biscuits. Spoon the apricot jam onto the remaining 12. Sift the icing sugar over the cut-out biscuits and use these to cover the jam-topped biscuits, pressing down gently.

crunchy nut & honey sandwiches

Makes about 30

Difficulty: Medium

Prep: 25 mins, plus cooling
Cook: 10–15 mins

INGREDIENTS

300 g/10½ oz unsalted
  butter, softened

140 g/5 oz caster sugar

1 egg yolk, lightly beaten

2 tsp vanilla extract

280 g/10 oz plain flour

pinch of salt

40 g/1½ oz macadamia nuts,
  cashew nuts or pine nuts,
  chopped

85 g/3 oz icing sugar

85 g/3 oz set honey

STEP 1. Preheat the oven to 190°C/375°F/Gas Mark 5. Line two large baking trays with baking paper.

STEP 2. Put 225 g/8 oz of the butter and the caster sugar into a mixing bowl and cream together until light and fluffy, then beat in the egg yolk and vanilla extract. Sift the flour and salt into the mixture and stir until combined.

STEP 3. Scoop up tablespoons of the dough and roll into balls. Place half of the balls on one of the prepared trays, spaced well apart, and flatten gently. Spread out the nuts in a shallow dish and dip one side of the remaining dough balls into them, then place on the other baking tray coated side up and flatten gently.

STEP 4. Bake in the preheated oven for 10–15 minutes, or until light golden brown. Leave to cool on the baking trays for 5–10 minutes, then transfer to wire racks and leave to cool completely.

STEP 5. Put the remaining butter, the icing sugar and honey into a bowl and beat together until creamy. Spread the honey mixture over the plain cookies and top with the nut-coated cookies.

shortbread

Makes 8

Difficulty: Medium

Prep: 20 mins, plus cooling
Cook: 45–50 mins

INGREDIENTS

175 g/6 oz plain flour,
 plus extra for dusting

pinch of salt

55 g/2 oz caster sugar,
 plus extra for sprinkling

115 g/4 oz unsalted butter,
 cut into small pieces, plus
 extra for greasing

STEP 1. Preheat the oven to 150°C/300°F/Gas Mark 2. Grease a 20-cm/8-inch fluted tart tin.

STEP 2. Put the flour, salt and sugar into a mixing bowl and stir to combine. Rub the butter into the dry ingredients. Continue to work the mixture until a soft dough forms. Do not overwork the shortbread or it will be tough, not crumbly as it should be.

STEP 3. Lightly press the dough into the prepared tin. Mark into eight pieces with a knife. Prick all over with a fork and bake in the preheated oven for 45–50 minutes until the shortbread is firm and just coloured.

STEP 4. Leave to cool in the tin and sprinkle with sugar. Carefully cut into slices along the marked lines and transfer to a wire rack to cool completely.

coconut macaroons

Makes 8

Difficulty: Medium

Prep: 25 mins, plus cooling
Cook: 15–20 mins

INGREDIENTS

2 large egg whites

115 g/4 oz caster sugar

150 g/5½ oz desiccated coconut

8 glacé cherries

STEP 1. Preheat the oven to 180°C/350°F/Gas Mark 4. Line two large non-stick baking trays with rice paper.

STEP 2. Put the egg whites into a large bowl and whisk until they hold soft peaks but are not dry. Add the sugar to the egg whites and, using a large metal spoon, fold in until incorporated. Add the coconut and fold in.

STEP 3. Place 4 heaped tablespoons of the mixture on each of the prepared trays and place a cherry on top of each macaroon.

STEP 4. Bake in the preheated oven for 15–20 minutes, or until light golden brown around the edges. Transfer to a wire rack to cool completely.

*Note: Not to be confused with the jewel-coloured French macaroons, these light yet chewy biscuits are a real teatime treat. If you don't have non-stick baking trays line them with baking paper, otherwise the rice paper, an integral part of the macaroon experience, will stick to the trays.

cherry garlands

Makes about 30

Difficulty: Medium

Prep: 20–25 mins, plus cooling
Cook: 8–10 mins

INGREDIENTS

150 g/5½ oz unsalted butter, softened

50 g/1¾ oz icing sugar

½ tsp vanilla extract

150 g/5½ oz plain flour

pinch of salt

70 g/2½ oz glacé cherries, finely chopped

STEP 1. Preheat the oven to 190°C/375°F/Gas Mark 5.

STEP 2. Put the butter and sugar into a mixing bowl and cream together until light and fluffy. Add the vanilla extract and beat until combined. Sift in the flour and salt in batches, mixing well between each addition. Add the cherries and mix well.

STEP 3. Spoon the mixture into a piping bag fitted with a 2.5-cm/1-inch star nozzle and pipe rings onto two large baking trays.

STEP 4. Bake in the preheated oven for 8–10 minutes, or until light golden. Transfer to a wire rack to cool.

*Note: These classic biscuits are perfect for dunking in a cup of coffee or tea. If you're not fond of glacé cherries, you could substitute dried cherries, or even dried cranberries or raisins.

melting moments

Makes 64

Difficulty: Medium

Prep: 20 mins, plus cooling
Cook: 15–20 mins

INGREDIENTS

350 g/12 oz unsalted butter, softened

85 g/3 oz icing sugar

½ tsp vanilla extract

300 g/10½ oz plain flour

50 g/1¾ oz cornflour

STEP 1. Preheat the oven to 180°C/350°F/Gas Mark 4. Line two large baking trays with baking paper.

STEP 2. Put the butter and icing sugar into a mixing bowl and cream together until light and fluffy, then beat in the vanilla extract. Sift the flour and cornflour into the bowl and mix together.

STEP 3. Spoon the mixture into a piping bag fitted with a large star nozzle and pipe 32 cookies onto each prepared tray, spaced well apart.

STEP 4. Bake in the preheated oven for 15–20 minutes, or until golden brown. Leave to cool on the trays.

*Note: These classic vanilla biscuits get lovely texture from the cornflour. Ring the flavour changes by substituting orange or lemon extract for the vanilla.

chocolate-dipped viennese fingers

Makes about 16

Difficulty: Medium

Prep: 25 mins, plus cooling and setting
Cook: 15–20 mins

INGREDIENTS

100 g/3½ oz unsalted butter,
 plus extra for greasing

25 g/1 oz golden caster
 sugar

½ tsp vanilla extract

100 g/3½ oz self-raising flour

100 g/3½ oz plain chocolate

STEP 1. Preheat the oven to 160°C/325°F/Gas Mark 3. Lightly grease two baking trays.

STEP 2. Put the butter, sugar and vanilla extract into a mixing bowl and cream together until pale and fluffy. Stir in the flour, mixing evenly to a fairly stiff dough.

STEP 3. Put the dough into a piping bag fitted with a large star nozzle and pipe about 16 fingers, each 6 cm/2½ inches long, onto the prepared trays.

STEP 4. Bake in the preheated oven for 10–15 minutes until pale golden. Leave to cool on the baking trays for 2–3 minutes, then use a palette knife to transfer to a wire rack and leave to cool completely.

STEP 5. Meanwhile, put the chocolate into a small heatproof bowl set over a saucepan of gently simmering water and heat until melted. Remove from the heat. Dip the ends of each biscuit into the chocolate to coat, then place on a sheet of baking paper and leave to set.

zesty almond biscotti

Makes about 20

Difficulty: Medium

Prep: 25 mins, plus cooling
Cook: 45–50 mins

INGREDIENTS

butter, for greasing

280 g/10 oz plain flour,
  plus extra for dusting

1 tsp baking powder

150 g/5½ oz caster sugar

85 g/3 oz blanched almonds

2 large eggs, lightly beaten

finely grated rind and juice
  of 1 lemon

STEP 1. Preheat the oven to 180°C/350°F/Gas Mark 4. Grease a large baking tray.

STEP 2. Sift the flour and baking powder into a mixing bowl. Add the sugar, almonds, eggs and lemon rind and juice to the flour and mix together to form a soft dough. Turn out the dough onto a lightly floured work surface and, with floured hands, knead for 2–3 minutes, or until smooth.

STEP 3. Divide the dough in half and shape each piece into a log shape with a diameter of about 4 cm/1½ inches. Place the logs on the prepared tray and flatten them to a thickness of 2.5 cm/1 inch.

STEP 4. Bake in the preheated oven for 25 minutes, or until light golden brown. Remove from the oven and leave to cool for 15 minutes. Reduce the oven temperature to 150°C/300°F/Gas Mark 2.

STEP 5. Using a serrated knife, cut the baked dough into 1-cm/½-inch thick slices and place cut side down on two baking trays. Bake for 10 minutes. Turn and bake for a further 10–15 minutes, or until golden brown and crisp. Transfer to a wire rack and leave to cool and harden.

pistachio & almond tuiles

Makes about 12

Difficulty: Medium

Prep: 25 mins, plus cooling
Cook: 10–15 mins

INGREDIENTS

1 egg white

55 g/2 oz golden caster
  sugar

25 g/1 oz plain flour

25 g/1 oz pistachio nuts,
  finely chopped

25 g/1 oz ground almonds

½ tsp almond extract

40 g/1½ oz unsalted butter,
  melted and cooled

STEP 1. Preheat the oven to 160°C/325°F/Gas Mark 3.
Line two baking trays with baking paper.

STEP 2. Put the egg white and sugar into a mixing bowl
and lightly whisk, then stir in the flour, pistachio nuts,
ground almonds, almond extract and butter and mix to a
soft paste.

STEP 3. Spoon walnut-sized heaps of the mixture on the
prepared trays and use the back of the spoon to spread
as thinly as possible. Bake in the preheated oven for
10–15 minutes until pale golden.

STEP 4. Quickly lift each biscuit with a palette knife and
place over the side of a rolling pin to shape into a curve.
When set, transfer to a wire rack to cool.

*Note: Speed is of the essence when curving the tuiles over the rolling pin. If they have set too hard they will crack, so just return them to the oven for 20–30 seconds to soften.

brandy snaps

Makes about 20

Difficulty: Hard

Prep: 30 mins, plus cooling
Cook: 35–40 mins

INGREDIENTS

85 g/3 oz unsalted butter

85 g/3 oz golden caster
  sugar

3 tbsp golden syrup

85 g/3 oz plain flour

1 tsp ground ginger

1 tbsp brandy

finely grated rind of
  ½ lemon

FILLING

150 ml/5 fl oz double cream
  or whipping cream

1 tbsp brandy (optional)

1 tbsp icing sugar

STEP 1. Preheat the oven to 160°C/325°F/Gas Mark 3. Line three large baking trays with baking paper.

STEP 2. Put the butter, caster sugar and golden syrup into a saucepan and heat over a low heat, stirring occasionally, until melted. Remove from the heat and leave to cool slightly. Sift the flour and ginger into the pan and beat until smooth, then stir in the brandy and lemon rind.

STEP 3. Drop small spoons of the mixture onto the prepared trays, spaced well apart. Place one tray at a time in the preheated oven for 10–12 minutes, or until golden brown.

STEP 4. Remove the first tray from the oven and leave to cool for about 30 seconds, then lift each brandy snap with a palette knife and wrap it around the handle of a wooden spoon. If the brandy snaps start to become too firm to wrap, return them to the oven for about 30 seconds to soften. When firm, remove from the spoon handles and transfer to a wire rack to cool completely. Repeat with the remaining brandy snaps.

STEP 5. To make the filling, whip the cream with the brandy, if using, and icing sugar until thick. Just before serving, pipe a little of the cream mixture into each end of the brandy snaps.

chocolate-dipped finger rolls

Makes about 35

Difficulty: Hard

Prep: 30 mins, plus 8 hours chilling, and cooling and setting
Cook: 17–20 mins

INGREDIENTS

250 g/9 oz icing sugar

125 g/4½ oz plain flour

pinch of salt

6 large egg whites

1 tbsp double cream

1 tsp vanilla extract

125 g/4½ oz unsalted butter, melted and cooled

125 g/4½ oz plain chocolate, chopped

STEP 1. Sift the icing sugar, flour and salt into a mixing bowl. Put the egg whites into a separate bowl and lightly whisk, then stir in the cream, vanilla extract and butter, then pour into the dry ingredients and mix until smooth. Cover and chill overnight in the refrigerator.

STEP 2. Preheat the oven to 200°C/400°F/Gas Mark 6.

STEP 3. Spoon tablespoons of the batter onto large baking trays. Using the back of a spoon, spread thinly into ovals 13 cm/5 inches long, spaced well apart. Bake in the preheated oven for 5–6 minutes, or until just browning at the edges. You will need to bake the batches one at a time.

STEP 4. Using a palette knife, take a cookie and roll it around the handle of a wooden spoon to make a cigarette shape. Transfer to a wire rack to cool and repeat with the remaining cookies.

STEP 5. When the finger rolls are cold, put the chocolate into a heatproof bowl set over a saucepan of gently simmering water and heat until melted. Dip one end of each roll into the chocolate, then place on a wire rack to set, with the coated end hanging over the edge.

desserts

white chocolate coffee gateau

Serves 8–10

Difficulty: Medium

Prep: 30 mins, plus 30 mins chilling, and cooling
Cook: 35–40 mins

INGREDIENTS

40 g/1½ oz unsalted butter,
  plus extra for greasing

85 g/3 oz white chocolate,
  broken into pieces

125 g/4½ oz caster sugar

4 large eggs, beaten

2 tbsp very strong black
  coffee

1 tsp vanilla extract

125 g/4½ oz plain flour

white chocolate curls,
  to decorate

FROSTING

175 g/6 oz white chocolate,
  broken into pieces

85 g/3 oz unsalted butter

125 g/4½ oz crème fraîche

125 g/4½ oz icing sugar,
  sifted

1 tbsp coffee liqueur or very
  strong black coffee

STEP 1. Preheat the oven to 180°C/350°F/Gas Mark 4. Grease two 20-cm/8-inch sandwich tins and line the bases with baking paper.

STEP 2. Put the butter and chocolate into a heatproof bowl set over a saucepan of gently simmering water and heat until just melted. Lightly stir to mix, then remove from the heat.

STEP 3. Put the caster sugar, eggs, coffee and vanilla extract into a separate heatproof bowl set over a saucepan of gently simmering water and whisk vigorously with a hand-held electric mixer until the mixture is pale and thick enough to leave a trail when the beaters are lifted. Remove from the heat, sift in the flour and fold in lightly. Quickly fold in the chocolate mixture, then divide between the prepared tins.

STEP 4. Bake in the preheated oven for 25–30 minutes until risen and golden. Leave to cool in the tins for 2 minutes, then turn out onto a wire rack to cool completely.

STEP 5. To make the frosting, put the chocolate and butter into a heatproof bowl set over a saucepan of gently simmering water and heat until melted. Remove from the heat and stir in the crème fraîche, icing sugar and liqueur. Chill for at least 30 minutes until thick and glossy. Use about one third of the frosting to sandwich the cakes together. Spread the remainder over the top and sides, then decorate with chocolate curls.

chocolate & almond layer cake

Serves 10–12

Difficulty: Medium

Prep: 35 mins, plus cooling
Cook: 35–40 mins

INGREDIENTS

7 eggs

200 g/7 oz caster sugar

150 g/5½ oz plain flour

50 g/1¾ oz cocoa powder

50 g/1¾ oz unsalted butter,
  melted, plus extra for
  greasing

FROSTING

200 g/7 oz plain chocolate,
  broken into pieces

125 g/4½ oz unsalted butter

50 g/1¾ oz icing sugar

TO DECORATE

75 g/2¾ oz toasted flaked
  almonds, lightly crushed

40 g/1½ oz milk chocolate,
  grated

STEP 1. Preheat the oven to 180°C/350°F/Gas Mark 4. Grease a 23-cm/9-inch square cake tin and line the base with baking paper.

STEP 2. Put the eggs and caster sugar in a mixing bowl and whisk with a hand-held electric mixer for about 10 minutes, or until the mixture is pale and thick enough to leave a trail when the beaters are lifted.

STEP 3. Sift together the flour and cocoa into a separate mixing bowl and fold half into the mixture. Drizzle over the melted butter, then fold in the remaining flour and cocoa mixture. Pour into the prepared tin and bake in the preheated oven for 30–35 minutes, or until springy to the touch. Leave to cool slightly, then remove from the tin and transfer to a wire rack to cool completely.

STEP 4. To make the frosting, put the chocolate and butter into a heatproof bowl set over a saucepan of gently simmering water and heat until melted, then remove from the heat. Stir in the icing sugar. Leave to cool, then beat until thick enough to spread.

STEP 5. Halve the cake lengthways and cut each half into three layers. Sandwich the layers together with three quarters of the filling. Spread the remainder over the cake, then press the almonds onto the sides and decorate the top with the grated chocolate.

blueberry swirl gateau

Serves 8–10

Difficulty: Medium

Prep: 40 mins, plus cooling
Cook: 20–25 mins

INGREDIENTS

oil or melted butter,
  for greasing

175 g/6 oz plain flour

1 tbsp baking powder

175 g/6 oz unsalted butter,
  softened

175 g/6 oz caster sugar

3 eggs, beaten

1 tsp orange flower water

2 tbsp orange juice

FROSTING

200 g/7 oz full-fat soft cheese

100 g/3½ oz icing sugar,
  sifted

225 g/8 oz fresh blueberries

STEP 1. Preheat the oven to 160°C/325°F/Gas Mark 3. Grease three 19-cm/7½-inch sandwich tins and line the bases with baking paper.

STEP 2. Sift the flour and baking powder into a mixing bowl and add the butter, caster sugar, eggs and orange flower water. Beat well until smooth, then stir in the orange juice.

STEP 3. Spoon the mixture into the prepared tins and smooth the surfaces with a palette knife. Bake in the preheated oven for 20–25 minutes, or until risen, firm and golden brown.

STEP 4. Leave to cool in the tins for 2–3 minutes, then turn out onto a wire rack and leave to cool completely.

STEP 5. To make the frosting, put the soft cheese and icing sugar into a mixing bowl and beat together until smooth. Transfer about two thirds of the mixture to a separate bowl, then stir in 140 g/5 oz of the blueberries. Use this to sandwich the cakes together.

STEP 6. Rub the remaining blueberries through a fine sieve to make a smooth purée. Spread the remaining frosting on top of the cake and swirl the blueberry purée through it.

pineapple hummingbird cake

Serves 8–10

Difficulty: Medium

Prep: 35 mins, plus cooling
Cook: 20–25 mins

INGREDIENTS

oil or melted butter,
  for greasing

175 g/6 oz plain flour

1 tbsp baking powder

1 tsp ground cinnamon

175 g/6 oz caster sugar

175 ml/6 fl oz sunflower oil

3 eggs, beaten

1 tsp vanilla extract

55 g/2 oz pecan nuts, finely
  chopped

2 small ripe bananas,
  mashed

85 g/3 oz canned crushed
  pineapple, drained

pineapple pieces and pecan
  nuts, to decorate

FROSTING

175 g/6 oz full-fat soft cheese

55 g/2 oz unsalted butter,
  softened

1 tsp vanilla extract

400 g/14 oz icing sugar,
  sifted

STEP 1. Preheat the oven to 180°C/350°F/Gas Mark 4. Grease three 23-cm/9-inch sandwich tins and line the bases with baking paper.

STEP 2. Sift the flour, baking powder and cinnamon into a mixing bowl and add the caster sugar, oil, eggs and vanilla extract. Beat well until smooth, then stir in the chopped pecan nuts, bananas and crushed pineapple.

STEP 3. Divide the mixture between the prepared tins, spreading evenly. Bake in the preheated oven for 20–25 minutes, or until risen, firm and golden brown.

STEP 4. Leave to cool in the tins for 2–3 minutes, then turn out onto a wire rack and leave to cool completely.

STEP 5. To make the frosting, put the soft cheese, butter, vanilla extract and icing sugar into a mixing bowl and beat together until smooth. Sandwich the cakes together with about two thirds of the mixture. Spread the remainder on top of the cake, then decorate with pineapple pieces and pecan nuts.

meringue-topped coffee liqueur cake

Serves 8–10

Difficulty: Medium

Prep: 35 mins, plus 2–3 mins cooling
Cook: 40–50 mins

INGREDIENTS

oil or melted butter,
  for greasing

175 g/6 oz plain flour

1 tbsp baking powder

175 g/6 oz unsalted butter,
  softened

175 g/6 oz light muscovado
  sugar

3 eggs, beaten

1 tsp coffee extract

2 tbsp milk

3 tbsp coffee liqueur

MERINGUE TOPPING

3 egg whites

150 g/5½ oz caster sugar

1½ tsp coffee extract

STEP 1. Preheat the oven to 160°C/325°F/Gas Mark 3. Grease a 25-cm/10-inch round cake tin and line with baking paper.

STEP 2. Sift together the flour and baking powder into a mixing bowl and add the butter, muscovado sugar, eggs and coffee extract. Beat well until smooth, then stir in the milk.

STEP 3. Spoon the mixture into the prepared tin and smooth the surface with a palette knife. Bake in the preheated oven for 40–50 minutes, or until risen, firm and golden brown.

STEP 4. Leave to cool in the tin for 2–3 minutes, then turn out onto a flameproof serving plate. Prick all over with a skewer, then sprinkle with the liqueur.

STEP 5. To make the meringue topping, put the egg whites into a clean, grease-free bowl and whisk with a hand-held electric mixer until soft peaks hold. Gradually add the caster sugar, whisking vigorously after each addition, then whisk in the coffee extract.

STEP 6. Spread the meringue on top of the cake. Use a chef's blowtorch to brown the meringue or place the cake under a hot grill for 2–3 minutes, or until just browned but still soft inside.

mango & ginger roulade

Serves 6

Difficulty: Hard

Prep: 45 mins, plus cooling
Cook: 15–20 mins

INGREDIENTS

oil or melted butter,
 for greasing

150 g/5½ oz plain flour

1½ tsp baking powder

175 g/6 oz unsalted butter,
 softened

175 g/6 oz golden caster
 sugar, plus extra for
 sprinkling

3 eggs, beaten

1 tsp vanilla extract

2 tbsp orange juice

1 large ripe mango

3 tbsp chopped glacé ginger

5 tbsp crème fraîche

STEP 1. Preheat the oven to 180°C/350°F/Gas Mark 4. Grease a 23 x 33-cm/9 x 13-inch Swiss roll tin and line with baking paper, leaving an overhang of 1 cm/½ inch. Lay a sheet of baking paper on the work surface and sprinkle with sugar.

STEP 2. Sift the flour and baking powder into a mixing bowl and add the butter, sugar, eggs and vanilla extract. Beat well until smooth, then beat in the orange juice.

STEP 3. Spoon the mixture into the prepared tin. Bake in the preheated oven for 15–20 minutes, or until risen, firm and golden brown.

STEP 4. Meanwhile, peel, stone and finely chop the mango. Put it into a small bowl and stir in the glacé ginger.

STEP 5. When cooked, turn out the sponge onto the sugared baking paper and spread with most of the mango mixture. Firmly roll up the sponge from a short side to enclose the filling, keeping the paper around the outside to hold it in place. Lift onto a wire rack to cool, removing the paper when firm.

STEP 6. When cold, top with spoonfuls of crème fraîche and decorate with the remaining mango mixture.

sachertorte

Serves 10

Difficulty: Medium

Prep: 40 mins, plus cooling and setting

Cook: 1 hour 10 minutes–1 hour 25 minutes

INGREDIENTS

175 g/6 oz plain chocolate, broken into pieces

140 g/5 oz unsalted butter, plus extra for greasing

140 g/5 oz caster sugar

6 eggs, separated

175 g/6 oz plain flour, sifted

fresh strawberries, to serve

ICING & FILLING

225 g/8 oz plain chocolate, broken into pieces

5 tbsp cold strong black coffee

115 g/4 oz icing sugar, sifted

6 tbsp apricot jam, warmed

STEP 1. Preheat the oven to 150°C/300°F/Gas Mark 2. Grease a 23-cm/9-inch round springform cake tin and line the base with baking paper.

STEP 2. Put the chocolate into a heatproof bowl set over a saucepan of gently simmering water and heat until melted. Remove from the heat and leave to cool slightly. Put the butter and half the caster sugar into a mixing bowl and cream together until pale and fluffy. Add the egg yolks and beat well. Add the chocolate, beating well. Fold in the flour. Whisk the egg whites in a separate bowl until soft peaks hold. Add the remaining caster sugar and whisk until stiff and glossy. Fold half into the chocolate mixture, then fold in the remainder.

STEP 3. Spoon into the prepared tin and smooth the surface. Bake in the preheated oven for 1–1¼ hours, or until a skewer inserted into the centre comes out clean. Leave to cool slightly in the tin, then transfer to a wire rack and leave to cool completely. Cut into two layers.

STEP 4. To make the icing, melt 175 g/6 oz of the chocolate as above and beat in the coffee. Whisk in the icing sugar until thick. Sandwich together the cake layers with the jam. Spoon over the icing, spreading to coat the top and sides. Leave to set for at least 2 hours.

STEP 5. Melt the remaining chocolate and spoon into a piping bag fitted with a fine plain nozzle. Pipe 'Sachertorte' on top of the cake. Leave to set. Serve with strawberries.

walnut torte

Serves 8–10

Difficulty: Medium

Prep: 35–40 mins, plus cooling
Cook: 25–30 mins

INGREDIENTS

oil or melted butter,
  for greasing

175 g/6 oz plain flour

1 tbsp baking powder

175 g/6 oz unsalted butter,
  softened

175 g/6 oz golden caster
  sugar

3 eggs, beaten

1 tsp vanilla extract

2 tbsp milk

125 g/4½ oz walnuts, finely
  chopped, plus extra walnut
  halves to decorate

3 tbsp apricot jam, warmed

FROSTING

175 g/6 oz unsalted butter

350 g/12 oz icing sugar,
  sifted

100 ml/3½ fl oz single cream

STEP 1. Preheat the oven to 180°C/350°F/Gas Mark 4. Grease two 20-cm/8-inch sandwich tins and line the bases with baking paper.

STEP 2. Sift the flour and baking powder into a mixing bowl and add the butter, caster sugar, eggs and vanilla extract. Beat well until smooth, then stir in the milk and 40 g/1½ oz of the chopped walnuts.

STEP 3. Divide the mixture between the prepared tins and smooth the surfaces with a palette knife. Bake in the preheated oven for 25–30 minutes, or until risen, firm and golden brown.

STEP 4. Leave to cool in the tins for 2–3 minutes, then turn out onto a wire rack and leave to cool completely. Slice each cake in half horizontally, making four layers in total.

STEP 5. To make the frosting, put the butter, icing sugar and cream into a mixing bowl and beat together until smooth. Spread about half the frosting over the top of three of the cakes and sandwich them together, placing the plain cake on top. Spread half the remaining frosting over the sides of the cake and press the remaining chopped walnuts over it.

STEP 6. Brush the jam over the top of the cake. Spoon the remaining frosting into a piping bag fitted with a star nozzle and pipe swirls around the top. Decorate with walnut halves.

sticky toffee cake

Serves 4

Difficulty: Easy

Prep: 30 mins
Cook: 40–45 mins

INGREDIENTS

75 g/2¾ oz sultanas

150 g/5½ oz stoned dates, chopped

1 tsp bicarbonate of soda

25 g/1 oz unsalted butter, plus extra for greasing

200 g/7 oz soft dark brown sugar

2 eggs

200 g/7 oz self-raising flour, sifted

STICKY TOFFEE SAUCE

25 g/1 oz unsalted butter

175 ml/6 fl oz double cream

200 g/7 oz soft dark brown sugar

STEP 1. Put the sultanas, dates and bicarbonate of soda into a heatproof bowl. Cover with boiling water and leave to soak.

STEP 2. Meanwhile, preheat the oven to 180°C/350°F/Gas Mark 4. Grease an 18-cm/7-inch square cake tin.

STEP 3. Put the butter and sugar into a mixing bowl and cream together. Beat in the eggs, then fold in the flour. Drain the sultanas and dates, add to the bowl and mix.

STEP 4. Spoon the mixture evenly into the prepared tin. Bake in the preheated oven for 35–40 minutes, or until a skewer inserted into the centre comes out clean.

STEP 5. About 5 minutes before the end of the cooking time, make the sauce. Melt the butter in a saucepan over a medium heat. Stir in the cream and sugar and bring to the boil, stirring constantly. Reduce the heat and simmer for 5 minutes.

STEP 6. Cut the cake into squares and turn out onto serving plates. Pour over the sauce and serve.

toffee apple upside-down cake

Serves 6

Difficulty: Medium

Prep: 35 mins, plus 2–3 mins cooling
Cook: 40–50 mins

INGREDIENTS

oil or melted butter,
  for greasing

175 g/6 oz plain flour

1 tbsp baking powder

175 g/6 oz unsalted butter,
  softened

175 g/6 oz caster sugar

3 eggs, beaten

1 tsp vanilla extract

finely grated rind of 1 lemon

TOFFEE APPLE TOPPING

55 g/2 oz unsalted butter

100 g/3½ oz caster sugar

1 tbsp water

4 eating apples

2 tbsp lemon juice

STEP 1. Preheat the oven to 180°C/350°F/Gas Mark 4. Grease a 23-cm/9-inch round cake tin.

STEP 2. To make the topping, put the butter and sugar into a heavy-based saucepan with the water and heat gently until melted, then bring to the boil. Reduce the heat and cook, stirring, until it is a deep golden caramel colour. Pour quickly into the prepared tin, tilting to cover the base evenly.

STEP 3. Peel, core and thickly slice the apples, toss with the lemon juice and spread evenly over the base of the tin.

STEP 4. Sift the flour and baking powder into a mixing bowl and add the butter, sugar, eggs and vanilla extract. Beat well until smooth, then stir in the lemon rind.

STEP 5. Spoon the mixture over the apples and smooth the surface with a palette knife. Bake in the preheated oven for 40–50 minutes, or until risen and golden brown.

STEP 6. Leave to cool in the tin for 2–3 minutes, then turn out carefully onto a warmed serving plate.

new york cheesecake

Serves 10

Difficulty: Easy

Prep: 30 mins, plus 2 hours cooling and setting, and 8 hours chilling
Cook: 1 hour

INGREDIENTS

100 g/3½ oz unsalted butter,
  plus extra for greasing

150 g/5½ oz digestive
  biscuits, finely crushed

1 tbsp granulated sugar

900 g/2 lb cream cheese

250 g/9 oz caster sugar

2 tbsp plain flour

1 tsp vanilla extract

finely grated rind of
  1 orange

finely grated rind of
  1 lemon

3 eggs

2 egg yolks

300 ml/10 fl oz double cream

STEP 1. Preheat the oven to 180°C/350°F/Gas Mark 4. Grease a 23-cm/9-inch round springform cake tin.

STEP 2. Put the butter into a small saucepan over a low heat and heat until melted. Remove from the heat, stir in the crushed biscuits and granulated sugar and mix thoroughly. Press the biscuit mixture into the base of the prepared tin. Bake in the preheated oven for 10 minutes. Remove from the oven and leave to cool. Increase the oven temperature to 200°C/400°F/Gas Mark 6.

STEP 3. Meanwhile, put the cream cheese in a food processor, and process until smooth, then gradually add the caster sugar and flour and process again until smooth. Increase the speed and add the vanilla extract, orange rind and lemon rind, then add the eggs and egg yolks, one at a time. Add the cream and process until smooth and combined.

STEP 4. Pour the filling into the tin. Smooth the top, transfer to the oven and bake for 15 minutes, then reduce the oven temperature to 110°C/225°F/Gas Mark ¼ and bake for a further 30 minutes. Switch off the oven and leave the cheesecake in it for 2 hours to cool and set. Cover and chill in the refrigerator overnight.

STEP 5. Slide a knife around the edge of the tin, then unclip and remove the springform. Cut the cake into slices and serve.

strawberry shortcake

Serves 8

Difficulty: Easy

Prep: 25 mins, plus cooling
Cook: 15 mins

INGREDIENTS

175 g/6 oz self-raising flour

100 g/3½ oz unsalted butter, diced and chilled, plus extra for greasing

75 g/2¾ oz caster sugar

1 egg yolk

1 tbsp rosewater

600 ml/1 pint whipping cream, lightly whipped

225 g/8 oz strawberries, hulled and quartered, plus a few whole strawberries to decorate

icing sugar, for dusting

STEP 1. Preheat the oven to 190°C/375°F/Gas Mark 5. Grease two baking trays and line with baking paper.

STEP 2. Sift the flour into a mixing bowl. Rub in the butter with your fingertips until the mixture resembles breadcrumbs. Stir in the caster sugar, then add the egg yolk and rosewater and mix to a soft dough.

STEP 3. Divide the dough in half. Roll out each piece into a 19-cm/7½-inch round and transfer to the prepared trays. Crimp the edges of the dough and prick all over with a fork.

STEP 4. Bake in the preheated oven for 15 minutes until light golden in colour. Transfer the shortcakes to a wire rack to cool.

STEP 5. Mix the cream with the strawberry quarters and spoon on top of one of the shortcakes. Cut the remaining round into wedges, then place on top of the cream. Dust with icing sugar and decorate with some whole strawberries.

apple pie

Serves 6

Difficulty: Medium

Prep: 40 mins, plus 30 mins chilling
Cook: 50 mins

INGREDIENTS

PASTRY

350 g/12 oz plain flour

pinch of salt

85 g/3 oz unsalted butter or
 margarine, cut into small
 pieces

85 g/3 oz lard or white
 vegetable fat, cut into small
 pieces

about 6 tbsp cold water

beaten egg or milk,
 for glazing

FILLING

750 g–1 kg/1 lb 10 oz–2 lb
 4 oz cooking apples,
 peeled, cored and sliced

125 g/4½ oz soft light brown
 sugar or caster sugar, plus
 extra for sprinkling

½–1 tsp ground cinnamon,
 mixed spice or ginger

1–2 tbsp water, if needed

STEP 1. To make the pastry, sift the flour and salt into a mixing bowl. Add the butter and lard and rub in with your fingertips until the mixture resembles fine breadcrumbs. Add the water and mix to a dough. Wrap in clingfilm and chill in the refrigerator for 30 minutes.

STEP 2. Preheat the oven to 220°C/425°F/Gas Mark 7. Roll out almost two thirds of the pastry to a thin round and use to line a 23-cm/9-inch pie plate or pie tin.

STEP 3. To make the filling, mix the apples with the sugar and cinnamon and pack into the pastry case. Add the water if needed, particularly if the apples are not very juicy. Roll out the remaining pastry to form a lid. Dampen the rim of the pie with water and position the lid, pressing the edges firmly together. Trim the edges.

STEP 4. Cut the trimmings into leaves or other shapes to decorate the top of the pie. Dampen and attach. Glaze the top of the pie with beaten egg, make a few slits in the top to allow the steam to escape during baking, then place on a baking sheet.

STEP 5. Bake in the preheated oven for 20 minutes, then reduce the oven temperature to 180°C/350°F/Gas Mark 4 and bake for a further 30 minutes, or until the pastry is a light golden brown. Serve hot or cold, sprinkled with sugar.

lemon & passion fruit tart

Serves 8

Difficulty: Medium

Prep: 45 mins, plus 40 mins chilling, and cooling
Cook: 45–50 mins

INGREDIENTS

PASTRY

200 g/7 oz plain flour,
  plus extra for dusting

pinch of salt

115 g/4 oz unsalted butter,
  chilled and diced

25 g/1 oz icing sugar,
  plus extra for dusting

1 egg yolk, blended with
  2 tbsp ice-cold water

FILLING

4 passion fruit, plus extra
  to decorate

juice and finely grated rind
  of 1 lemon

150 ml/5 fl oz double cream

4 tbsp crème fraîche

85 g/3 oz caster sugar

2 eggs

2 egg yolks

STEP 1. To make the pastry, sift the flour and salt into a mixing bowl. Rub in the butter with your fingertips until the mixture resembles fine breadcrumbs. Stir in the icing sugar and blended egg yolk and mix to a dough. Turn onto a floured work surface and knead until smooth. Wrap in clingfilm and chill in the refrigerator for 20 minutes.

STEP 2. Preheat the oven to 200°C/400°F/Gas Mark 6 and preheat a baking sheet. Roll out the pastry on a lightly floured surface and use to line a 23-cm/9-inch loose-based fluted tart tin. Chill for 20 minutes.

STEP 3. Prick the pastry base all over, line with baking paper and fill with dried beans. Place on the preheated baking sheet and bake for 10 minutes, then remove the paper and beans and return the pastry case to the oven for a further 5 minutes until light golden. Reduce the oven temperature to 180°C/350°F/Gas Mark 4.

STEP 4. To make the filling, halve the passion fruit and scoop out the seeds and pulp into a fine sieve set over a jug. Press with the back of a spoon until you have about 75 ml/2½ fl oz juice. Whisk together the passion fruit juice, lemon juice and rind, cream, crème fraîche, caster sugar, eggs and egg yolks until smooth. Pour into the pastry case. Bake for 30–35 minutes until just set. Leave to cool completely. To serve, dust with icing sugar and decorate with passion fruit seeds and pulp.

sweet pumpkin pie

Serves 6–8

Difficulty: Medium

Prep: 40 mins, plus 30 mins chilling
Cook: 2 hours 20 mins

INGREDIENTS

FILLING

1.8 kg/4 lb pumpkin, quartered and deseeded
400 ml/14 fl oz condensed milk
2 eggs
1 tsp salt
½ tsp vanilla extract
1 tbsp demerara sugar

PASTRY

140 g/5 oz plain flour, plus extra for dusting
¼ tsp baking powder
1½ tsp ground cinnamon
¾ tsp ground nutmeg
¾ tsp ground cloves
50 g/1¾ oz caster sugar
55 g/2 oz unsalted butter, chilled and diced, plus extra for greasing
1 egg, beaten

TOPPING

2 tbsp plain flour
4 tbsp demerara sugar
1 tbsp ground cinnamon
25 g/1 oz unsalted butter, chilled and diced
85 g/3 oz pecan nuts, chopped
70 g/2½ oz walnuts, chopped

STEP 1. Preheat the oven to 190°C/375°F/Gas Mark 5. To make the filling, place the pumpkin quarters skin side up in a roasting tin and cover with foil. Bake in the preheated oven for 1½ hours. Scoop out the flesh and purée in a food processor. Drain off any excess liquid, then cover the purée and chill in the refrigerator.

STEP 2. Meanwhile, grease a 23-cm/9-inch pie dish. To make the pastry, sift the flour and baking powder into a mixing bowl. Stir in the spices and caster sugar. Rub in the butter with your fingertips until the mixture resembles breadcrumbs, then add the egg and mix to a dough. Turn out onto a lightly floured work surface, roll out and use to line the prepared dish. Cover and chill in the refrigerator for 30 minutes.

STEP 3. Preheat the oven to 220°C/425°F/Gas Mark 7. Put the pumpkin purée into a large bowl, then stir in the condensed milk and eggs. Stir in the salt, vanilla extract and demerara sugar. Pour into the pastry case and bake in the preheated oven for 15 minutes.

STEP 4. Meanwhile, make the topping. Combine the flour, demerara sugar and cinnamon, then rub in the butter until crumbly and stir in the nuts. Remove the pie from the oven and reduce the oven temperature to 180°C/350°F/Gas Mark 4. Sprinkle over the topping, then bake for a further 35 minutes. Serve warm or cold.

pecan pie

Serves 8

Difficulty: Medium

Prep: 40 mins, plus 30 mins chilling
Cook: 50–55 mins

INGREDIENTS

PASTRY

200 g/7 oz plain flour,
  plus extra for dusting

115 g/4 oz unsalted butter

2 tbsp caster sugar

FILLING

70 g/2½ oz unsalted butter

100 g/3½ oz light muscovado
  sugar

140 g/5 oz golden syrup

2 large eggs, beaten

1 tsp vanilla extract

115 g/4 oz pecan nuts

STEP 1. To make the pastry, put the flour into a mixing bowl and rub in the butter with your fingertips until it resembles fine breadcrumbs. Stir in the caster sugar and add enough cold water to mix to a firm dough. Wrap in clingfilm and chill in the refrigerator for 15 minutes, or until firm enough to roll out.

STEP 2. Preheat the oven to 200°C/400°F/Gas Mark 6. Roll out the pastry on a lightly floured surface and use to line a 23-cm/9-inch loose-based tart tin. Prick the base with a fork. Chill for 15 minutes.

STEP 3. Place the tart tin on a baking sheet, line with baking paper and fill with dried beans. Bake in the preheated oven for 10 minutes, then remove the paper and beans and bake for a further 5 minutes. Reduce the oven temperature to 180°C/350°F/Gas Mark 4.

STEP 4. To make the filling, put the butter, muscovado sugar and golden syrup into a saucepan and heat gently until melted. Remove from the heat and quickly beat in the eggs and vanilla extract.

STEP 5. Roughly chop the pecan nuts and stir into the mixture. Pour into the pastry case and bake for 35–40 minutes until the filling is just set. Serve warm or cold.

summer fruit tartlets

Makes 12

Difficulty: Medium

Prep: 45 mins, plus 30 mins chilling, and cooling
Cook: 15–20 mins

INGREDIENTS

PASTRY

200 g/7 oz plain flour,
  plus extra for dusting

85 g/3 oz icing sugar

55 g/2 oz ground almonds

115 g/4 oz unsalted butter,
  diced and chilled

1 egg yolk

1 tbsp milk

FILLING

275 g/9¾ oz cream cheese

icing sugar, to taste,
  plus extra for dusting

350 g/12 oz fresh
  mixed berries, such as
  blueberries, raspberries and
  strawberries

STEP 1. To make the pastry, sift the flour and icing sugar into a mixing bowl, then stir in the ground almonds. Rub in the butter with your fingertips until the mixture resembles breadcrumbs. Add the egg yolk and milk and mix to a firm dough. Turn out onto a lightly floured work surface and knead briefly. Wrap the dough in clingfilm and chill in the refrigerator for 30 minutes.

STEP 2. Preheat the oven to 200°C/400°F/Gas Mark 6.

STEP 3. Roll out the pastry and use it to line 12 deep tartlet or individual brioche tins. Prick the pastry bases with a fork. Press a piece of foil into each tartlet, covering the edges, and bake in the preheated oven for 10–15 minutes, or until light golden brown. Remove the foil and bake for a further 2–3 minutes. Transfer the pastry cases to a wire rack to cool.

STEP 4. To make the filling, put the cream cheese and icing sugar into a mixing bowl and mix well. Put a spoonful of filling into each pastry case and arrange the berries on top. Dust with icing sugar and serve immediately.

apple strudel with cider sauce

Serves 2–4

Difficulty: Medium

Prep: 35 mins
Cook: 25–30 mins

INGREDIENTS

8 eating apples

1 tbsp lemon juice

115 g/4 oz sultanas

1 tsp ground cinnamon

½ tsp ground nutmeg

1 tbsp soft light brown sugar

6 sheets filo pastry, thawed if
  frozen

vegetable oil spray

SAUCE

1 tbsp cornflour

450 ml/16 fl oz dry cider

STEP 1. Preheat the oven to 190°C/375°F/Gas Mark 5. Line a baking tray with baking paper.

STEP 2. Peel and core the apples and chop them into 1-cm/½-inch dice. Toss the apples in a bowl with the lemon juice, sultanas, cinnamon, nutmeg and brown sugar.

STEP 3. Lay out a sheet of filo pastry on the work surface, spray with oil and lay a second sheet on top. Repeat with a third sheet. Spread over half the apple mixture and roll up lengthways, tucking in the ends to enclose the filling. Repeat with the remaining filo pastry and filling to make a second strudel. Slide onto the prepared baking tray, spray with oil and bake in the preheated oven for 15–20 minutes, or until golden.

STEP 4. To make the sauce, blend the cornflour in a saucepan with a little cider until smooth. Add the remaining cider and heat gently, stirring, until the mixture boils and thickens. Serve the strudel warm or cold accompanied by the cider sauce.

strawberry cream cobbler

Serves 4

Difficulty: Medium

Prep: 30 mins
Cook: 30–40 mins

INGREDIENTS

800 g/1 lb 12 oz strawberries,
  hulled and halved

50 g/1¾ oz caster sugar

clotted cream, to serve

COBBLER TOPPING

200 g/7 oz self-raising flour,
  plus extra for dusting

pinch of salt

40 g/1½ oz unsalted butter

2 tbsp caster sugar

1 egg, beaten

25 g/1 oz sultanas

25 g/1 oz currants

about 5 tbsp milk, plus extra
  for glazing

STEP 1. Preheat the oven to 200°C/400°F/Gas Mark 6.

STEP 2. Arrange the strawberries evenly in the bottom of an ovenproof dish, sprinkle over the sugar and cook in the preheated oven for 5–10 minutes until heated through.

STEP 3. Meanwhile, to make the cobbler topping, sift the flour and salt into a large mixing bowl. Rub in the butter with your fingertips until the mixture resembles fine breadcrumbs, then stir in the sugar. Add the egg, sultanas and currants, and mix lightly until incorporated. Stir in enough of the milk to make a smooth dough.

STEP 4. Transfer to a lightly floured work surface and lightly knead, then roll out to a thickness of about 1 cm/½ inch. Cut out rounds using a 5-cm/2-inch biscuit cutter. Arrange the dough rounds over the strawberries, then brush the tops with a little milk.

STEP 5. Bake in the preheated oven for 25–30 minutes, or until the cobbler topping has risen and is light golden in colour. Serve hot with clotted cream.

apple & blackberry crumble

Serves 4

Difficulty: Easy

Prep: 30 mins
Cook: 40–45 mins

INGREDIENTS

900 g/2 lb cooking apples

300 g/10½ oz blackberries,
fresh or frozen

55 g/2 oz light muscovado
sugar

1 tsp ground cinnamon

CRUMBLE TOPPING

85 g/3 oz self-raising white
flour

85 g/3 oz plain wholemeal
flour

115 g/4 oz unsalted butter

55 g/2 oz demerara sugar

STEP 1. Preheat the oven to 190°C/375°F/Gas Mark 5.

STEP 2. Peel and core the apples and cut into chunks. Put into a mixing bowl with the blackberries, muscovado sugar and cinnamon and mix together, then transfer to an ovenproof baking dish.

STEP 3. To make the crumble topping, sift the white flour into a bowl and stir in the wholemeal flour. Add the butter and rub it in with your fingertips until the mixture resembles fine breadcrumbs. Stir in the demerara sugar.

STEP 4. Spread the crumble over the apple mixture and bake in the preheated oven for 40–45 minutes, or until the apples are soft and the crumble topping is golden brown and crisp.

*Note: This is the perfect dessert to make after a Sunday afternoon blackberry-picking expedition. Serve with ice cream or mascarpone cheese for a real treat.

bread & savouries

irish soda bread

Makes 1 loaf

Difficulty: Easy

Prep: 20 mins
Cook: 25–30 mins

INGREDIENTS

butter, for greasing

450 g/1 lb plain flour,
    plus extra for dusting

1 tsp salt

1 tsp bicarbonate of soda

400 ml/14 fl oz buttermilk

STEP 1. Preheat the oven to 220°C/425°F/Gas Mark 7. Lightly grease a baking tray.

STEP 2. Sift the flour, salt and bicarbonate of soda into a mixing bowl. Make a well in the centre of the dry ingredients and pour in most of the buttermilk.

STEP 3. Mix well together using your hands. The dough should be very soft but not too wet. If necessary, add the remaining buttermilk.

STEP 4. Turn out the dough onto a lightly floured work surface and lightly knead, then shape it into a 20-cm/8-inch round.

STEP 5. Place on the prepared baking tray, cut a cross in the top and bake in the preheated oven for 25–30 minutes until golden brown and it sounds hollow when tapped on the base.

*Note: Soda bread needs a very light hand for mixing and kneading in order to keep the texture as airy as possible. Don't add all the buttermilk at once — too much will make the dough very sticky and give a poor result.

crusty white bread

Makes 1 loaf

Difficulty: Medium

Prep: 30 mins, plus 1½ hours proving, and cooling
Cook: 30 mins

INGREDIENTS

1 egg

1 egg yolk

500 g/1 lb 2 oz strong white
   flour, plus extra for dusting

1½ tsp salt

2 tsp sugar

1 tsp easy-blend dried yeast

25 g/1 oz butter, diced

sunflower oil, for oiling

STEP 1. Put the egg and egg yolk into a jug and lightly beat to mix. Add enough lukewarm water to make up to 300 ml/10 fl oz. Stir well.

STEP 2. Put the flour, salt, sugar and yeast into a large bowl. Add the butter and rub it in with your fingertips until the mixture resembles breadcrumbs. Make a well in the centre, add the egg mixture and work to a smooth dough.

STEP 3. Turn out onto a lightly floured work surface and knead well for about 10 minutes until smooth. Brush a bowl with oil. Shape the dough into a ball, place it in the bowl and cover with a damp tea towel. Leave to rise in a warm place for 1 hour until the dough has doubled in volume.

STEP 4. Oil a 900-g/2-lb loaf tin. Turn out the dough onto a lightly floured work surface and knead for 1 minute until smooth. Shape the dough into a piece the length of the tin and three times the width. Fold the dough in three lengthways and place it in the tin with the join underneath. Cover and leave to stand in a warm place for 30 minutes until it has risen above the rim of the tin.

STEP 5. Meanwhile, preheat the oven to 220°C/425°F/ Gas Mark 7. Bake the loaf in the preheated oven for 30 minutes, or until firm and it sounds hollow when tapped on the base. Transfer to a wire rack to cool.

wholemeal harvest bread

Makes 1 loaf

Difficulty: Medium

Prep: 30 mins, plus 1½ hours proving, and cooling
Cook: 30 mins

INGREDIENTS

225 g/8 oz strong wholemeal flour, plus extra for dusting

1 tbsp skimmed milk powder

1 tsp salt

2 tbsp soft light brown sugar

1 tsp easy-blend dried yeast

1½ tbsp sunflower oil, plus extra for oiling

175 ml/6 fl oz lukewarm water

STEP 1. Put the flour, milk powder, salt, sugar and yeast into a large bowl. Pour in the oil and add the water, then mix well to a smooth dough.

STEP 2. Turn out onto a lightly floured work surface and knead well for about 10 minutes until smooth. Brush a bowl with oil. Shape the dough into a ball, place it in the bowl and cover with a damp tea towel. Leave to rise in a warm place for 1 hour until the dough has doubled in volume.

STEP 3. Oil a 900-g/2-lb loaf tin. Turn out the dough onto a lightly floured work surface and knead for 1 minute until smooth. Shape the dough into a piece the length of the tin and three times the width. Fold the dough in three lengthways and place it in the tin with the join underneath. Cover and leave in a warm place for 30 minutes until it has risen above the rim of the tin.

STEP 4. Meanwhile, preheat the oven to 220°C/425°F/ Gas Mark 7. Place the loaf in the preheated oven and bake for 30 minutes, or until golden brown and it sounds hollow when tapped on the base. Transfer to a wire rack to cool.

blue cheese, fig & walnut bread

Makes 1 loaf

Difficulty: Medium

Prep: 25 mins, plus 30 mins soaking, and cooling
Cook: 55 mins

INGREDIENTS

85 g/3 oz dried figs, roughly
   chopped

4 tbsp Marsala

butter, for greasing

200 g/7 oz plain flour

1 tbsp baking powder

3 eggs

200 g/7 oz crème fraîche

175 g/6 oz blue cheese,
   such as Roquefort or
   Gorgonzola, crumbled

75 g/2¾ oz walnuts, roughly
   chopped

salt and pepper

STEP 1. Put the figs into a small bowl, pour over the Marsala and leave to soak for 30 minutes.

STEP 2. Preheat the oven to 180°C/350°F/Gas Mark 4. Lightly grease a 450-g/1-lb loaf tin and line with baking paper.

STEP 3. Sift the flour and baking powder into a mixing bowl. Put the eggs and crème fraîche into a separate mixing bowl and beat together until smooth. Stir the egg mixture into the flour mixture until well combined. Season to taste with salt and pepper.

STEP 4. Add 150 g/5½ oz of the cheese, all the figs and the Marsala, then stir in half the walnuts. Turn the mixture into the prepared tin, scatter over the remaining cheese and walnuts and bake in the preheated oven for 40 minutes, or until the loaf is golden brown.

STEP 5. Cover the tin loosely with foil and return to the oven for a further 15 minutes, or until a skewer inserted into the centre of the loaf comes out clean. Leave to cool in the tin for 5 minutes, then turn out onto a wire rack to cool completely.

muesli bread

Makes 1 loaf

Difficulty: Medium

Prep: 30 mins, plus 1 hour 30 mins–1 hour 40 minutes proving, and cooling
Cook: 30–35 mins

INGREDIENTS

300 g/10½ oz strong white flour, plus extra for dusting

85 g/3 oz strong wholemeal flour

1½ tsp salt

150 g/5½ oz unsweetened muesli

3 tbsp skimmed milk powder

1½ tsp easy-blend dried yeast

225 ml/8 fl oz lukewarm water

2 tbsp vegetable oil, plus extra for brushing

1 tbsp clear honey

70 g/2½ oz ready-to-eat dried apricots, chopped

STEP 1. Sift the white flour, wholemeal flour and salt into a mixing bowl, tipping in any bran left in the sieve. Stir in the muesli, milk powder and yeast. Make a well in the centre and pour in the water, oil and honey. Stir with a wooden spoon until the mixture begins to come together, then mix to a dough with your hands.

STEP 2. Turn out the dough onto a lightly floured work surface and knead well for 5 minutes. Add the apricots and knead for a further 5 minutes until the dough is smooth and elastic.

STEP 3. Brush a bowl with oil. Shape the dough into a ball, place it in the bowl and cover with clingfilm. Leave to rise in a warm place for 1 hour until the dough has doubled in volume.

STEP 4. Brush a baking tray with oil. Turn out the dough onto a lightly floured work surface and knock back with your fist. Shape the dough into a round and place on the prepared baking tray. Cut a cross in the top of the loaf. Cover the baking tray with a damp tea towel and leave to rise in a warm place for 30–40 minutes.

STEP 5. Meanwhile, preheat the oven to 200°C/400°F/Gas Mark 6. Bake the loaf in the preheated oven for 30–35 minutes until golden brown and it sounds hollow when tapped on the base. Transfer to a wire rack to cool.

olive & sun-dried tomato bread

Makes 2 loaves

Difficulty: Medium

Prep: 30 mins, plus 1 hour 45 mins–2 hours 15 mins proving, plus cooling
Cook: 40 mins

INGREDIENTS

400 g/14 oz plain flour,
  plus extra for dusting

1 tsp salt

7 g/¼ oz easy-blend dried
  yeast

1 tsp brown sugar

1 tbsp chopped fresh thyme

200 ml/7 fl oz lukewarm
  water

4 tbsp olive oil, plus extra for
  brushing

55 g/2 oz black olives,
  stoned and sliced

55 g/2 oz green olives,
  stoned and sliced

100 g/3½ oz sun-dried
  tomatoes in oil, drained
  and sliced

1 egg yolk, beaten

STEP 1. Sift together the flour and salt into a mixing bowl and stir in the yeast, sugar and thyme. Make a well in the centre and pour in the water and oil. Stir with a wooden spoon until the mixture begins to come together, then mix to a dough with your hands.

STEP 2. Turn out onto a lightly floured work surface and add the olives and sun-dried tomatoes, then knead for a 5 minutes until the dough is smooth and elastic.

STEP 3. Brush a bowl with oil. Shape the dough into a ball, place it in the bowl and cover with clingfilm. Leave to rise in a warm place for 1–1½ hours until the dough has doubled in volume.

STEP 4. Dust a baking tray with flour. Turn out the dough onto a lightly floured work surface and knock back. Cut it in half and shape each half into a round. Place the rounds on the prepared tray and cover with a damp tea towel. Leave to rise in a warm place for 45 minutes.

STEP 5. Meanwhile, preheat the oven to 200°C/400°F/ Gas Mark 6. Make three shallow diagonal slashes on the top of each loaf and brush with the egg yolk. Bake the loaves in the preheated oven for 40 minutes until golden brown and they sound hollow when tapped on the base. Transfer to a wire rack to cool.

tomato & rosemary focaccia

Makes 1 loaf

Difficulty: Medium

Prep: 30 mins, plus 3 hours proving, and cooling
Cook: 20 mins

INGREDIENTS

500 g/1 lb 2 oz strong white flour, plus extra for dusting

1½ tsp salt

1½ tsp easy-blend dried yeast

2 tbsp chopped fresh rosemary, plus extra sprigs to garnish

6 tbsp extra virgin olive oil, plus extra for brushing

300 ml/10 fl oz lukewarm water

6 oven-dried or sun-blush tomato halves, sliced

1 tsp coarse sea salt

STEP 1. Sift together the flour and salt into a mixing bowl and stir in the yeast and chopped rosemary. Make a well in the centre, pour in 4 tablespoons of the oil and mix with a wooden spoon. Gradually stir in the water – do not over-mix. Turn out the dough onto a lightly floured work surface and knead for 2 minutes. The dough will be quite wet, but do not add more flour.

STEP 2. Brush a bowl with oil. Shape the dough into a ball, put it into the bowl and cover with clingfilm. Leave to rise in a warm place for 2 hours until the dough has doubled in volume.

STEP 3. Brush a baking tray with oil. Turn out the dough onto a lightly floured work surface and knock back, then knead for 1 minute. Put the dough on the prepared tray and press out into an even layer. Cover the tray with a damp tea towel and leave to rise in a warm place for 1 hour.

STEP 4. Preheat the oven to 240°C/475°F/Gas Mark 9. Whisk the remaining oil with a little water in a bowl. Dip your fingers into the oil mixture and press them into the dough to make dimples all over. Sprinkle with the tomatoes, salt and rosemary sprigs. Reduce the oven temperature to 220°C/425°F/Gas Mark 7 and bake the focaccia for 20 minutes until golden brown. Transfer to a wire rack to cool slightly before serving.

corn bread

Makes 1 loaf

Difficulty: Easy

Prep: 20 mins, plus 5–10 mins cooling
Cook: 30–35 mins

INGREDIENTS

vegetable oil, for oiling

175 g/6 oz plain flour

1 tsp salt

4 tsp baking powder

1 tsp caster sugar

280 g/10 oz polenta

115 g/4 oz butter, softened

4 eggs

225 ml/8 fl oz milk

3 tbsp double cream

STEP 1. Preheat the oven to 200°C/400°F/Gas Mark 6. Oil a 20-cm/8-inch square cake tin.

STEP 2. Sift together the flour, salt and baking powder into a mixing bowl. Add the sugar and polenta and stir to mix. Add the butter and cut it into the dry ingredients with a knife, then rub it in with your fingertips until the mixture resembles breadcrumbs.

STEP 3. Lightly beat the eggs in a bowl with the milk and cream, then stir into the polenta mixture until thoroughly combined.

STEP 4. Spoon the mixture into the prepared tin and smooth the surface. Bake in the preheated oven for 30–35 minutes until a skewer inserted into the centre of the loaf comes out clean. Remove the tin from the oven and leave to cool for 5–10 minutes, then cut into squares and serve warm.

*Note: Corn bread has a delicious rustic texture and is great with hearty soups. You could ramp up the flavour by adding 140 g/5 oz grated mature Cheddar cheese and three finely chopped red or green chillies at the end of Step 3.

wholemeal cheddar scones

Makes 12

Difficulty: Medium

Prep: 20 mins, plus cooling
Cook: 10 mins

INGREDIENTS

sunflower oil, for oiling

225 g/8 oz self-raising
  wholemeal flour, plus extra
  for dusting

1 tsp English mustard
  powder

1 tsp salt

40 g/1½ oz butter, chilled
  and finely diced

115 g/4 oz mature Cheddar
  cheese, grated

2 tbsp snipped fresh chives

about 150 ml/5 fl oz milk,
  plus extra for glazing

STEP 1. Preheat the oven to 220°C/425°F/Gas Mark 7. Very lightly brush a baking tray with oil.

STEP 2. Put the flour, mustard powder and salt into a food processor and process until blended. Add the butter and quickly process until crumbs form, then stir in the cheese and chives and process again. Slowly add just enough milk to make a soft, light dough, taking care not to over-process the dough.

STEP 3. Turn out the dough onto a lightly floured work surface and pat out with a lightly floured rolling pin to a thickness of 2 cm/¾ inch. Handle the dough as little as possible. Use a 5-cm/2-inch round biscuit cutter to stamp out 12 scones, re-rolling the trimmings as necessary.

STEP 4. Place the scones on the prepared tray and brush the tops with milk. Bake in the preheated oven for 10 minutes, or until risen and golden brown on top. Transfer to a wire rack to cool.

chunky apple & cheese muffins

Makes 12

Difficulty: Easy

Prep: 25 mins, plus 5–10 mins cooling
Cook: 20–25 mins

INGREDIENTS

250 g/9 oz plain flour

1 tbsp baking powder

½tsp salt

4 tbsp sunflower oil

150 ml/5 fl oz low-fat natural
    yogurt

2 eggs, beaten

125 ml/4 fl oz milk

140 g/5 oz extra-mature
    Cheddar cheese, coarsely
    grated

2 dessert apples, cored and
    cut into 5-mm/¼-inch dice

55 g/2 oz sultanas

STEP 1. Preheat the oven to 190°C/375°F/Gas Mark 5. Line a 12-hole muffin tin with paper cases.

STEP 2. Sift the flour, baking powder and salt into a mixing bowl and make a well in the centre. Add the oil, yogurt, eggs and milk, then mix well to combine evenly.

STEP 3. Reserve about 2 tablespoons of the cheese and add the remainder to the bowl with the apples and sultanas, lightly stirring to mix.

STEP 4. Spoon the mixture into the paper cases and sprinkle with the reserved cheese. Bake in the preheated oven for 20–25 minutes, or until the muffins are well risen and golden brown.

STEP 5. Leave to cool in the tin for 5–10 minutes, then serve warm.

*Note: Muffins are very easy to make, and require very little mixing for the best results. You could replace the Cheddar cheese with Parmesan or Grana Padano for a tangy finish.

courgette & sesame seed muffins

Makes 12

Difficulty: Easy
Prep: 20 mins, plus 5 mins cooling
Cook: 20 mins

INGREDIENTS

melted butter,
 for greasing

300 g/10½ oz small firm
 courgettes

280 g/10 oz plain flour

1 tbsp baking powder

⅛ tsp salt

6 tsp sesame seeds

½ tsp dried mixed herbs

2 eggs

250 ml/9 fl oz buttermilk

6 tbsp sunflower oil

pepper

STEP 1. Preheat the oven to 200°C/400°F/Gas Mark 6. Grease a 12-hole muffin tin. Grate the courgettes, squeezing out any excess moisture.

STEP 2. Sift together the flour, baking powder and salt, with pepper to taste, into a mixing bowl. Stir in two thirds of the sesame seeds and all the herbs.

STEP 3. Lightly beat the eggs in a large jug or bowl, then beat in the buttermilk and oil. Make a well in the centre of the dry ingredients, pour in the beaten liquid ingredients and add the courgettes. Stir gently until just combined; do not over-mix.

STEP 4. Spoon the mixture into the prepared muffin tin. Scatter the remaining sesame seeds over the tops of the muffins. Bake in the preheated oven for about 20 minutes until well risen, golden brown and firm to the touch.

STEP 5. Leave the muffins to cool in the tin for 5 minutes, then serve warm.

italian pesto muffins

Makes 12

Difficulty: Easy

Prep: 20 mins, plus 5 mins cooling
Cook: 20 mins

INGREDIENTS

280 g/10 oz plain flour

1 tbsp baking powder

⅛ tsp salt

50 g/1¾ oz pine nuts

2 eggs

150 ml/5 fl oz buttermilk

6 tbsp sunflower oil

6 tbsp pesto

10 g/¼ oz freshly grated
   Parmesan cheese

pepper

STEP 1. Preheat the oven to 200°C/400°F/Gas Mark 6. Line a 12-hole muffin tin with paper cases.

STEP 2. Sift together the flour, baking powder and salt, with pepper to taste, into a mixing bowl. Add the pine nuts and stir to combine.

STEP 3. Lightly beat the eggs in a large jug or bowl, then beat in the buttermilk, oil and pesto. Make a well in the centre of the dry ingredients and pour in the beaten liquid ingredients. Stir gently until just combined; do not over-mix.

STEP 4. Spoon the mixture into the prepared tin. Scatter the cheese over the tops of the muffins. Bake in the preheated oven for about 20 minutes until well risen, golden brown and firm to the touch.

STEP 5. Leave the muffins to cool in the tin for 5 minutes, then serve warm.

savoury oat crackers

Makes 12–14

Difficulty: Easy

Prep: 20 mins, plus cooling
Cook: 12–15 mins

INGREDIENTS

90 g/3¼ oz porridge oats

25 g/1 oz wholemeal plain
    flour

100 g/3½ oz unsalted butter,
    plus extra for greasing

½ tsp coarse sea salt

1 tsp dried thyme

40 g/1½ oz walnuts, finely
    chopped

1 egg, beaten

40 g/1½ oz sesame seeds

STEP 1. Preheat the oven to 180°C/350°F/Gas Mark 4.
Lightly grease two baking trays.

STEP 2. Put the oats and flour into a mixing bowl and rub
in the butter with your fingertips. Stir in the salt, thyme
and walnuts, then add the egg and mix to a soft dough.

STEP 3. Spread out the sesame seeds on a large shallow
plate or tray. Break off walnut-sized pieces of dough and
roll into balls, then roll in the sesame seeds to coat lightly
and evenly.

STEP 4. Place the balls of dough on the prepared trays,
spaced well apart, and roll a rolling pin over them to
flatten them as much as possible. Bake in the preheated
oven for 12–15 minutes, or until firm and pale gold.

STEP 5. Leave to cool on the trays for 3–4 minutes, then
transfer to a wire rack and leave to cool completely.

cheese sablés

Makes about 35

Difficulty: Easy

Prep: 25 mins, plus 30 mins chilling, and cooling
Cook: 10 mins

INGREDIENTS

150 g/5½ oz plain flour,
  plus extra for dusting

150 g/5½ oz mature Cheddar
  cheese, grated

150 g/5½ oz butter, diced,
  plus extra for greasing

1 egg yolk

3 tbsp sesame seeds

STEP 1. Put the flour and cheese into a mixing bowl and mix together. Add the butter to the cheese and flour mixture and rub in with your fingertips until combined.

STEP 2. Stir in the egg yolk and mix to a dough. Wrap the dough in clingfilm and chill in the refrigerator for about 30 minutes.

STEP 3. Preheat the oven to 200°C/400°F/Gas Mark 6. Lightly grease several baking trays.

STEP 4. Thinly roll out the dough on a lightly floured work surface. Stamp out 6-cm/2½-inch rounds with a biscuit cutter, re-rolling and cutting the trimmings to make 35 rounds in total.

STEP 5. Place the rounds on the prepared trays and sprinkle the sesame seeds over them.

STEP 6. Bake in the preheated oven for 10 minutes until the sablés are light golden in colour. Carefully transfer to a wire rack and leave to cool slightly before serving.

cheese straws

Makes about 24

Difficulty: Easy

Prep: 20 mins, plus 30 mins chilling, and cooling
Cook: 10–15 mins

INGREDIENTS

115 g/4 oz plain flour,
  plus extra for dusting

pinch of salt

1 tsp curry powder

55 g/2 oz butter, plus extra
  for greasing

55 g/2 oz grated Cheddar
  cheese

1 egg, beaten

1 tbsp each poppy and
  cumin seeds

STEP 1. Sift the flour, salt and curry powder into a mixing bowl. Add the butter and rub it in with your fingertips until the mixture resembles breadcrumbs. Add the cheese and half the egg and mix to form a dough. Wrap in clingfilm and chill in the refrigerator for 30 minutes.

STEP 2. Preheat the oven to 200°C/400°F/Gas Mark 6. Grease two baking trays.

STEP 3. Roll out the dough on a floured work surface to a thickness of 5 mm/¼ inch thick. Cut into 7.5 x 1-cm/ 3 x ½-inch strips. Pinch the strips lightly along the sides and place them on the prepared trays.

STEP 4. Brush with the remaining egg and sprinkle half the strips with the poppy seeds and half with the cumin seeds. Bake in the preheated oven for 10–15 minutes, or until golden. Transfer to wire racks to cool.

*Note: A perennial favourite with adults and children alike, versatile cheese straws make great party canapés, tasty pre-dinner nibbles or moreish snacks with dips. You can vary the spices and seeds to taste.

quiche lorraine

Serves 6–8

Difficulty: Medium

Prep: 30 mins, plus 10 mins chilling and 10 mins cooling
Cook: 50–55 mins

INGREDIENTS

PASTRY

200 g/7 oz plain flour,
   plus extra for dusting

100 g/3½ oz butter

1–2 tbsp cold water

FILLING

15 g/½ oz butter

1 small onion, finely chopped

4 lean streaky bacon rashers,
   diced

55 g/2 oz Gruyère cheese or
   Cheddar cheese, grated

2 eggs, beaten

300 ml/10 fl oz single cream

pepper

STEP 1. To make the pastry, sift the flour into a mixing bowl and rub in the butter with your fingertips until the mixture resembles fine breadcrumbs. Stir in just enough of the water to make a firm dough.

STEP 2. Roll out the dough on a lightly floured work surface, then use to line a 23-cm/9-inch loose-based tart tin. Trim the edges and prick the base all over with a fork. Chill in the refrigerator for at least 10 minutes.

STEP 3. Preheat the oven to 200°C/400°F/Gas Mark 6 and preheat a baking tray. Line the pastry case with baking paper and fill with dried beans. Place on the tray and bake in the preheated oven for 10 minutes, then remove the paper and beans and bake for a further 10 minutes.

STEP 4. To make the filling, melt the butter in a frying pan, add the onion and bacon and cook over a medium heat for about 5 minutes. Spread evenly over the hot pastry case and sprinkle with half the cheese. Beat together the eggs and cream and season to taste with pepper. Pour into the pastry case and sprinkle with the remaining cheese.

STEP 5. Reduce the oven temperature to 190°C/375°F/Gas Mark 5. Place the quiche in the oven and bake for 25–30 minutes, or until golden brown and just set. Leave to cool in the tin for 10 minutes before turning out.

leek & onion tartlets

Makes 6

Difficulty: Medium

Prep: 30 mins, plus 30 mins chilling, and cooling
Cook: 45 mins

INGREDIENTS

butter, for greasing

225 g/8 oz ready-made
   shortcrust pastry

plain flour, for dusting

FILLING

25 g/1 oz unsalted butter

1 onion, thinly sliced

450 g/1 lb leeks, thinly sliced

2 tsp chopped fresh thyme

55 g/2 oz Gruyère cheese,
   grated

3 eggs

300 ml/10 fl oz double cream

salt and pepper

STEP 1. Lightly grease six 10-cm/4-inch tartlet tins. Roll out the pastry on a lightly floured work surface and stamp out six rounds with a 13-cm/5-inch biscuit cutter. Use to line the prepared tins, then trim the edges and prick the bases all over with a fork. Transfer to the refrigerator to chill for 30 minutes.

STEP 2. Preheat the oven to 190°C/375°F/Gas Mark 5. Line the pastry cases with foil and fill with dried beans, then place on a baking tray and bake in the preheated oven for 8 minutes. Remove the foil and beans and bake for a further 2 minutes. Transfer to a wire rack to cool. Reduce the oven temperature to 180°C/350°F/Gas Mark 4.

STEP 3. Meanwhile, make the filling. Melt the butter in a large, heavy-based frying pan. Add the onion and cook, stirring constantly, for 5 minutes, or until soft. Add the leeks and thyme and cook, stirring, for 10 minutes, or until soft. Divide the mixture between the pastry cases and sprinkle over the cheese.

STEP 4. Beat together the eggs and cream and season to taste with salt and pepper. Pour the mixture into the pastry cases and place on a baking tray. Bake for 15 minutes, or until golden brown and just set. Leave to cool slightly before turning out.

vegetable jalousie

Serves 4

Difficulty: Medium

Prep: 35 mins
Cook: 45–50 mins

INGREDIENTS

25 g/1 oz butter

1 leek, shredded

2 garlic cloves, crushed

50 g/1¾ oz mushrooms, sliced

1 red pepper, deseeded and sliced

1 yellow pepper, deseeded and sliced

75 g/2¾ oz small asparagus spears

2 tbsp plain flour, plus extra for dusting

6 tbsp vegetable stock

6 tbsp milk

4 tbsp dry white wine

1 tbsp chopped fresh oregano

450 g/1 lb ready-made puff pastry

1 egg, beaten

salt and pepper

STEP 1. Preheat the oven to 200°C/400°F/Gas Mark 6. Dampen a sheet of baking paper with water and use to line a baking tray.

STEP 2. Melt the butter in a saucepan. Add the leek and garlic and sauté for 2 minutes. Stir in the mushrooms, red pepper, yellow pepper and asparagus and cook for 3–4 minutes.

STEP 3. Add the flour and cook for 1 minute. Remove from the heat and stir in the stock, milk and wine. Return to the heat and bring to the boil, stirring, until thickened. Stir in the oregano and season with salt and pepper.

STEP 4. Roll out half the pastry on a lightly floured work surface to a 38 x 15-cm/15 x 6-inch rectangle. Roll out the other half into a slightly larger rectangle. Place the smaller rectangle on the prepared baking tray.

STEP 5. Spoon the filling on top of the smaller rectangle, leaving a 1-cm/½-inch margin all around. Cut parallel slits across the larger rectangle to within 2.5 cm/1 inch of the edges. Brush around the edges of the smaller rectangle with a little of the beaten egg and place the larger rectangle on top, sealing the edges well. Brush with the remaining beaten egg and bake in the preheated oven for 30–35 minutes until risen and golden.

mushroom & spinach parcels

Makes 4

Difficulty: Medium

Prep: 30 mins
Cook: 30–35 mins

INGREDIENTS

25 g/1 oz butter

1 red onion, halved and sliced

2 garlic cloves, crushed

225 g/8 oz open-cap mushrooms, sliced

175 g/6 oz baby spinach

pinch of nutmeg

4 tbsp double cream

225 g/8 oz ready-made puff pastry

plain flour, for dusting

1 egg, beaten

2 tsp poppy seeds

salt and pepper

STEP 1. Preheat the oven to 200°C/400°F/Gas Mark 6. Dampen a baking tray with water.

STEP 2. Melt the butter in a frying pan. Add the onion and garlic and sauté for 3–4 minutes until soft.

STEP 3. Add the mushrooms, spinach and nutmeg and cook for a further 2–3 minutes. Stir in the cream, mixing well. Season to taste with salt and pepper and remove the pan from the heat.

STEP 4. Roll out the pastry on a lightly floured work surface and cut into four 15-cm/6-inch rounds. Spoon a quarter of the filling onto half of each round and fold the pastry over to encase the filling. Press down to seal the edges of the pastry and brush with the beaten egg. Sprinkle with the poppy seeds.

STEP 5. Place the parcels on the prepared tray and cook in the preheated oven for 20 minutes until risen and golden brown.

STEP 6. Transfer the parcels to serving plates and serve immediately.

hot cheese pastries

Makes 32

Difficulty: Medium

Prep: 35 mins
Cook: 15 mins

INGREDIENTS

olive oil, for oiling

200 g/7 oz feta cheese

115 g/4 oz cottage cheese

3 tbsp chopped fresh
  flat-leaf parsley

2 eggs, beaten

8 sheets filo pastry

pepper

STEP 1. Preheat the oven to 190°C/375°F/Gas Mark 5. Oil two baking trays.

STEP 2. Crumble the feta cheese into a bowl. Add the cottage cheese, parsley and eggs and beat together with a fork until well blended. Season to taste with pepper.

STEP 3. Cut the filo pastry down the longest length, into four strips, each about 7 cm/2¾ inches wide. Take one strip and cover the remaining strips with a damp tea towel. Brush the strip with a little oil and put a heaped teaspoon of the cheese mixture on the bottom left-hand corner. Fold over the corner with the filling so that it meets the long side edge and forms a triangle. Continue folding the filling up and over from side to side to form a neat triangle. Place the triangle on a prepared tray and brush with oil. Continue until all the pastry strips and the filling have been used.

STEP 4. Bake the pastries in the preheated oven for about 15 minutes until golden brown. Serve hot.

Index